Opera, Orchids and Oz

Hazel Barker

Opera, Orchids and Oz
© Hazel Barker 2022

Published by Armour Books
P. O. Box 492, Corinda QLD 4075, Australia

Front cover photo: Fabien Bellanger / Unsplash | Description: pink moth orchid in bloom in close up photography.

Cover, interior design, typeset & orchid icon by Beckon Creative

ISBN: 978-1-925380-46-0

 A catalogue record for this book is available from the National Library of Australia

No part of this book may be reproduced, stored in a retrieval system or transmitted in any form or by any means, without the prior permission in writing of the publisher, nor be otherwise circulated in any form of binding or cover other than that in which it is published and without a similar condition, including this condition, being imposed on the subsequent purchaser.

Note: Australian spelling and grammatical conventions are used throughout this book.

~Dedication~

*This book is dedicated to my darling husband, Colin,
and
The surviving members of my family:
My sister, Maxine Rose O'Connell
and
My brother, Robin Winston White*

Preface

OPERA, ORCHIDS AND OZ is the final instalment of my memoirs, *Heaven Tempers the Wind: Story of a War Child* and its sequel, *The Sides of Heaven*. Both books have been finalists in the CALEB Competitions of 2017 and 2019 respectively.

Book One covers the period from the Japanese invasion of Burma in 1941 to the family's return to war-ravaged Rangoon after the war. Told through a child's eyes, it unfolds a family's travails during the darkest days of enemy occupation. Threaded with light, shot with hope, it recounts Hazel's hard-won passage from innocence to maturity.

Book Two, *The Sides of Heaven*, is set during the turbulent period following the Second World War and the subsequent civil wars. It is brutally honest, compelling and may be disturbing to some readers. From a family's endurance, a mother's faith and a young girl's traumatic journey through her teenage years intimately springs a story of redemption and hope. Hazel yearns for freedom, yet chooses life in a convent, she yearns for her family, yet spreads her wings for Australia.

Opera, Orchids and Oz continues with Hazel's life story as well as her family's that build-up from a meditation on grief to a splendid conclusion. It is the story of a grieving woman and her husband finding a new life after the loss of their baby, and discovering joy in opera, orchids and travel in Oz and overseas.

In conclusion, I would like to thank my dearly beloved husband Colin for his patience and help towards my writing career, and my writing groups for their invaluable critiques and suggestions during the creation of this book.

Contents

Chapter		Page
1	Man Proposes but God Disposes—*Thomas à Kempis*	9
2	That which does not kill, makes us stronger—*Nietzche*	23
3	Canberra, 1973–1974	31
4	My Family, 1973–1974	39
5	Canberra, 1975–1983	45
6	1974–1976	51
7	Queensland, 1976–1986	63
8	The Tyranny of Distance	75
9	Colin's Dad	87
10	Visits to Perth, 1993–1998	95
11	Opera, an Opiate, 1995–1998	99
12	1998–1999	109
13	2000–2003	119
14	2004	129
15	2004–2006	137
16	Farewell to Bertie, 2007	143
17	2008-2009	151
18	Milestones & Mishaps, 2010	161
19	2011	171
20	When One Door Closes, Another Opens, 2012	175
21	A Rewarding Year, 2013	179
22	More Milestones, 2014	187
23	Trials & Triumphs, 2015	193

24	Surprises, 2016	201
25	Falls, Family, Friends & Feasting, 2017	207
26	2018	215
27	Flooding, Fires & Ants, 2019	225
28	Panic, 2020	235
29	April to August 2020	245
30	September to December 2020	253
31	Epilogue	263

~ Chapter 1 ~

Man Proposes but God Disposes, Thomas à Kempis

FROM THE VERY FIRST MOMENT we met there was a strong chemistry between us. We were always on the same wavelength. I could not picture life without him. We wrote little notes to each other, leaving them all over the house. Our love grew stronger as the days went by. We had the same spirit of adventure, the same dream.

Ever since our marriage in February 1971, when the alarm woke us in the mornings, I would lie with my head resting on Colin's chest, listening to the rhythm of his heart. I would enjoy the warmth of his body before we said our prayers and had breakfast.

After our evening meal, we would relax and listen to music in the lounge. The unit in Queanbeyan was sparsely furnished, with no television, but I kept it neat and tidy and replenished the vase on the side table with fresh flowers. The sound of traffic faded away as we cuddled, lost in our own universe, often in silence, happy in our embraces; at other times sharing our plans before drifting off to sleep.

Colin was a Building Inspector in the Department of Works, Canberra. I was completing my final year for my Bachelor of Arts degree as an external student. The nuns at St. Pat's College, Braddon, had promised me a teaching position as soon as a vacancy occurred. I prayed it would soon happen. Meanwhile, I also applied for work as a clerk in the Public Service while taking a job as a kitchen maid.

This is only temporary, I told myself, as I choked over the stink of kitchen waste and struggled to prevent myself from dry retching. I kept looking at the clock, wishing its hands would move faster. In the evenings, Colin picked me up from work. The sight of him erased all my discomfort.

Fortunately, I did not remain a kitchen maid long. Within two months I had a clerical position in the Customs and Excise Department of the Public Service, and no longer held down a menial job with meagre wages. All our financial troubles were behind us. I was welcomed into the Public Service by Jenny and her friend John, who was sweet on her.

After work one evening, relaxing in the lounge room, Colin stroked my hair. 'We must buy a block of land and build a house before we have a family. I have a builder's licence and could erect a solid brick house. We have enough savings to buy the construction materials. We wouldn't be able to afford labourers, but I would like to start straight away.'

'You build a house for us all by yourself?'

'I helped Dad build our family home when I was only an apprentice.'

Thrilled at the prospect of having our own home, I clasped my hands. 'I'll help you!'

Colin hugged me. 'You can help mix the mortar.'

The next weekend we inspected the available blocks, and selected one in Darwinia Terrace, Rivett. On Monday, Colin paid $2,220 for the land, and commenced drawing a plan for our first home. To add to our savings, he worked even on Saturday mornings.

As soon as the Council approved our plans, we applied for a government loan.

The clerk lifted his brows in a condescending manner. 'Which firm will be constructing your house?' He tapped his pen on the counter.

'I'll be doing that myself. I'm a builder.'

I noted the pride in Colin's voice. *Now he cannot refuse us a loan.*

The clerk shrugged and filed our application with an air of finality. 'Well. Come back when you've reached lock-up stage.'

How can he refuse a loan when we are willing and capable to do all the work ourselves?

Colin reached for my hand and we stormed out of the office.

The next weekend, Colin commenced digging the house foundations with a pick, while I shovelled dirt into a barrow. He hired a workmate to help him finish. 'From now on we will not be able to afford any holiday until the house is completed.'

I nodded, but still simmered with anger for not being granted a loan.

Colin taught me how to operate a concrete mixer, and how to mix the sand with the cement. Then he hosed enough water into the mixture to give it the right texture. He laid the bricks and poured the wet concrete around them to give the house a solid foundation. It was back-breaking work, yet he built the walls brick-by-brick. He was used to hard work, but I had never done manual labour. My muscles ached for days.

Each Saturday after work, we had lunch at the site, then continued laying bricks. Colin's father, Albert, who worked in the Department of Parks and Gardens, also finished at noon. He and Colin's mother, Eva, would drop in after lunch. She expected us to entertain them, and interrupted us with her incessant talking. It irritated me, so I stayed at our flat to catch up on my studies as my university exams were fast approaching.

One afternoon, Eva knocked at our door, but I pretended to be out, and did not answer. 'Hazel, Hazel are you there?' she called out. 'It's Mum.'

Why can't she leave me in peace? I need time to study. I remained quiet and tried to ignore her. Perhaps I should have opened the door and let her in, because I could not concentrate on my work with her constant knocking and calling out. She finally left.

After that full day of hard work, Colin returned, looking worried. 'Mum said she called, and you weren't at home.'

'I purposely didn't answer the door. I stayed home to study and didn't have the time to entertain her.'

Colin looked relieved, but she was his mother so I suspect he was hurt. I shook with anger, wondering whether she was attempting to undermine our marriage. 'Is she trying to drive a wedge between us by arousing your distrust?'

Was she annoyed because I had taken her son away from her? I thought of my mother's unhappy marriage. Of my father's groundless suspicions. Of the brutality and beatings. *Our marriage must be built on love, on trust and on fidelity. I must never, ever let anyone come between us.*

'She always blows hot and cold,' Colin said. 'She likes to rule people's lives, but she will never rule ours. Why do you suppose I chose to build at the other end of town?'

I hugged him, knowing I would be wearing his dirt and dust afterwards. Then we laughed, and Colin had a well-needed shower before dinner.

Colin laid the foundations from below ground to two feet above ground, to floor level. 'That's one third of all the brick laying done. It is so important to build a solid foundation.'

This is how our marriage must be, I thought. *A solid foundation and it will last forever.*

One Saturday, when Colin's parents visited our site, his father helped to install a large window. After that, my resentment towards Eva was slightly mollified. My anger simmered down, because I knew Albert could never have done it without her consent.

When the exterior walls were completed, Colin erected the roof trusses by himself. I will never forget the sight of him standing on the wall, drawing them up with a rope, shoring each one with planks, and getting it to straddle the walls. After he had installed the trusses, we engaged a roof tiler. Colin then commenced constructing the framework for the house. I admired his versatility. He had done all the brickwork by himself and now I witnessed his carpentry skills.

After my exams at the Australian National University, I could assist Colin even more, but we exhausted our savings in ten months, so work on the house came to a halt. From the outside, it looked like a fully built home, but it remained a hollow shell. Exactly as I felt. Hollow and hopeless.

When I passed the exams, the government reimbursed my fees, and I was promoted to Graduate Clerk. What a blessing! The cheque of $650 paid for the plasterer, the plumber, and the electrician. It brought the house to lock up stage, and we were granted the loan. Now we had the money to finish the house. A load dropped from our shoulders.

While Colin kept busy painting the walls, his father laid the tiles in the wet areas. Our ideal home was nearing completion. My wildest dreams were coming true.

Life had never been a bed of roses for me. My happy childhood had been cut short when the Japanese had entered Burma in 1941 and, within a few years, I lost my eldest brother and sister. Then, my father made our lives a misery until we fled and took shelter in a convent. Later, when Burma attained independence from Britain in January 1948, civil war broke out, and I fled to Australia. Now, I had found love, and we were going to start a family.

Whenever we spoke of having a baby, Colin said, 'First things first. We must finish the house.'

We had been practising the Rhythm or the Billings Method of contraception, the only birth control system allowed by our church. It had been difficult for both of us. By Christmas, we decided it was time to start a family. Soon, I was carrying Colin's child, and our baby was due in September 1972.

'Our baby will be a boy and look like you.' I smoothed my dress over my stomach.

'Could be a girl who looks like you,' Colin teased. He hoped to complete the house before our baby was born, so we could move into our new home.

I made sure not to do anything strenuous. Anything that would harm the baby. One Sunday however, I fell off the verandah and landed on my stomach. I instantly thought of the baby and clasped my belly, while Colin dropped his paint brush and raced to me.

'I hope baby is all right,' I gasped.

'Do you feel pain?' Colin asked.

'No pain at all but poor baby took the brunt of the fall.'

'Go and lie down, and from now on, you must not do any work,' Colin said.

After that, he only let me do light jobs like passing nails to him or helping tidy up when it grew too dark to work.

A month before my due date, I developed a loud, hacking cough. I would spread my palms beneath my belly to protect our baby from the tremors that shook my body. Each time I had a coughing fit, a look of concern crossed Colin's face and fear clutched my heart. He made an appointment for me with our general practitioner, who prescribed a course of penicillin tablets.

On our return home from the surgery, I took the first dose. Within minutes, I rushed to the bathroom and vomited. A sour smell arose. I rinsed my mouth and washed the mess down the sink. Colin rubbed my back and brought me a glass of water, then he raced to the phone and told the GP what had happened.

'Don't worry. I'll send a nurse around to give her a penicillin injection,' he replied.

An hour crept by. A nurse came and administered a needle. After she left, my skin grew red and angry. I broke out in a rash.

'It itches and burns.' My throat felt tight, my voice was high pitched. I collapsed on the bed.

Colin phoned our doctor again.

'Take her to hospital immediately!' The doctor's voice boomed over the phone.

Colin drove me to Canberra's only hospital. In less than half an hour, I lapsed into a semi-conscious state, barely aware of a nurse putting me to bed. There I lay, tossing from side to side, unable to distinguish between reality and nightmares. I dreamt of someone moaning, and when I awoke, I was not sure if it had been me or someone else. Once, I remember climbing out of bed, falling on the floor, and blacking out. The sound of running footsteps woke me. A nurse put me back into bed and scolded me for not pressing a bell to summon her. Then I lost consciousness.

I vaguely recall Colin stroking my hair, but drained of strength, I lay inert, unable to even move my lips. My periods of unconsciousness were interspersed by brief periods of rationality. One afternoon, someone must have drawn the curtains, because a shaft of sunlight pierced my eyes.

A voice whispered, 'You've lost your baby.'

'My baby has been born?' My voice sounded weak and hoarse.

'Well, you gave birth and the baby's dead.'

Although my eyes were open, I could not distinguish anything but light and shadow. I did not know who was speaking because I could not see clearly, but I later found it was the young resident doctor. Like a cold steel blade, grief pierced my soul. *Impossible! Our baby could not have left us.* I checked my stomach. No longer firm and round, but soft and squishy, nothing moved beneath my touch. *The baby I had nurtured within my body for eight months is now no more.* Fear gripped me. Pain stabbed the back of my throat. *Is this a terrible nightmare? Where are you, Colin? We've lost our baby. Did the little one look like you? We'll never hear it laugh or cry or hold the precious bundle in our arms.* I lapsed into merciful unconsciousness...

In a haze of grief and medication, interrupted by doctors and specialists more interested in my vital signs than my state of mind, I remained in bed, numb with grief. I felt I was walking in the dark and feeling my way ahead.

When Colin came to see me after our baby's funeral, I recognised him for the first time, and flung my arms around him. 'I haven't seen you for so long!'

'Been with you every day,' he assured me. 'I sent for your mother and met her at the airport... She's waiting outside.'

Mum entered. A look of unutterable suffering spread over her face as soon as she saw me. Her puffy eyes showed she had not slept.

That night, Colin took Mum to the village of Hall, where she stayed with his parents. In August, darkness descended early, and the nights were still cold. In the mornings, Colin drove through the frosty countryside to pick her up and drop her off at the hospital. Mum would sit beside me and pray, passing a glass of water whenever I needed it. I drew comfort from her presence but could not express my feelings of appreciation. I felt too weak to talk much. Pain wracked my body. Pain tore at my left side. Pain enveloped my chest at every breath. I spent most of the day dozing.

After another five days in Intensive Care, the doctor removed the drip. Then I was shifted to another private ward.

As soon as Dr Goulston assured Mum the crisis was over, she bent down and said, 'Now that you're on the mend, do you mind if I return to Perth? It's freezing here.'

I detected her pleading tone and shuddered at the thought of her leaving me. I laid my hand on her arm. 'Stay a bit longer. The days will grow warmer now that spring is here.'

But Mum had left England because of the harsh weather. Now the cold was driving her away from me, even though spring impatiently peered around the corner.

She left for Perth the next day. My heart ached. She had left me just when my health was improving, and I could communicate without dozing off.

The following day, the hospital chaplain spoke words of comfort. 'Ask the Lord to heal your wounds. Pray for strength to bear the loss of your child. Remember that Mary lost her child too. She understands just how you feel.'

My mother had always instilled in me the love of the Virgin Mary. I called upon her to intercede for me, and asked God for strength. Both moral and physical. His healing grace fell on me like raindrops. I felt stronger. *Perhaps my health will return, and we'll be able to raise a family one day?*

With Mum gone, the days were long. I yearned for the evenings when Colin would visit. My throat was so dry; I could only whisper. My muscles had weakened so much I barely had the strength to walk the short distance to the toilet and shower.

I do not recall my GP coming to see me. However the liver specialist, Doctor Goulston, visited daily to check on my progress.

One morning, seeing that my voice was still scarcely audible, he said, 'If you can't speak any louder, I'll have to send a speech therapist to see you.' His words sounded like a threat. Or was it a challenge?

I tried reading aloud after he left. The words came out like a child learning to read for the first time—slow and halting. With perseverance, however, my voice improved, but my speech remained slow and my voice soft for months after my illness.

The ache in my chest persisted for weeks. I stood up and attempted a stretch, hoping to alleviate the pain. When I raised my arms to a vertical position, a wave of agony surged through me. Then a sudden flood of air inflated my lungs and the pain vanished.

When I told Dr Goulston about it, he advised me to make an appointment for further x-rays at his clinic after my discharge.

One evening, I begged Colin to tell me everything while I had been unconscious. His words poured out. 'You would not eat or drink. The nurses asked me to get you to take liquids, but you bared your teeth at me like a rabid dog and refused. When I held the cup to your mouth, you bit me. A nurse told me there was nothing more I could do.'

I heard his panic as he re-lived the scene. Frustrated at my helplessness, Colin had continued going to work. Every night when he left the hospital, he hoped and prayed all would be well. Whenever possible, while driving around inspecting buildings, he had dropped in at the hospital. At nights, he returned home and cooked his meal.

'The food tasted like dust. My stomach churned.' His voice was soft and casual, as if reluctant to let me know his distress. 'On your tenth day in hospital, I received a phone call from a nurse who told me that you had entered labour, so I raced to be at your side. When

I arrived at the hospital, I was left waiting outside the room. I had expected to hold your hand and comfort you during your delivery, but they shut me out. After several hours in the labour ward, the doctor came out to meet me. "Congratulations. You have a baby girl and all's well."'

I listened, breathless while Colin continued. 'I held out a trembling hand and grasped his outstretched one. I felt like sharing my joy with the world, so I rushed to the Post Office and sent off a wire to Perth, conveying the good news to your mother. Then I hurried back to the hospital. Once there, I strode past the reception room, up the lifts and along the corridors until I reached the delivery room. I knocked at the door, hoping to see you and the baby. A nurse opened the door a chink, her eyes wide in surprise, but she would not let me in. I just exploded. "Why am I not allowed to see my wife? The GP told me that everything is all right! What's happening to Hazel? To the baby? The baby is premature. Is she fully formed?" I clenched my hands to prevent myself from throttling her. She shut the door in my face.

'Hours later, the resident doctor came out and strode towards me. "Your wife is unwell," he said. "I've placed a drip in her arm and I'm sending for a hepatologist." The intern's gruff manner didn't worry me. All I wanted was to know exactly what was going on behind those doors. The suspense proved unbearable. I sprang to my feet and entered the room. Several figures in masks and hospital gowns milled around, but once again, the nurses barred my way and ushered me outside. I longed to barge in again, despite their protests, but fearing to cause further harm to you, I let myself be led out, then collapsed onto a chair. I waited and waited, feeling all alone in the world.'

My jaw hung open. *What an ordeal he had been through!*

'A doctor dashed into the room and remained there for what seemed like ages,' Colin went on. 'Sometime later, he came out. "I'm Dr Goulston, a hepatologist. I am sorry to tell you that both mother and child have jaundice. If your wife lives through this, she may be a semi-invalid and never lead a normal life. The baby, too, has only a slender chance of surviving. She has a brain haemorrhage. I have given her a blood transfusion and she is in a humidicrib." He gave my arm a sympathetic squeeze and left. When I was finally allowed to enter your room, you tossed and turned in bed, unaware of my presence. I'll never forget those glazed eyes. I had no one to turn to. No one to confide in. No one to share my problems.'

Colin went on to say that, numbed by pain and distress, it had never entered his mind to phone his parents about the baby's birth. A desert of wilderness stretched before him. God seemed to have abandoned him.

He dreaded what the future would bring. Stumbling on, blinded by pain, his mind in turmoil, he lost count of time. Shattered, he went on to automatic pilot. The precise details of those days remain a blank. He remembers phoning Gem Ballantyne, my friend and colleague in Perth. 'Please buy a return plane ticket to Canberra for Hazel's mother. I'll send a cheque to cover the costs. Hazel only has a slim chance of recovery.'

He must have phoned his parents eventually, because he recalled a nurse conducting him and his mother to see our baby. She lay in a humidicrib, and all Colin could see was a mass of dark hair. The rest of her body was covered by a blanket. He never got to hold her. The fruit of our love. Our flesh and blood.

'After my parents left, I stood helpless and looked around. I rubbed my nose, hoping to erase the smell of antiseptic that permeated the room. Overcome by grief, the weight of my sorrow was like a grindstone that crushed every ounce of joy out of me. Then someone came up, placed a hand upon my shoulder and asked whether I'd like to have the baby baptised. He wore a black cassock and held a prayer book in his hands. In my agony, I hadn't thought of getting our baby christened. I knew you would want it, and want it urgently, as we were in danger of losing her. I nodded, unable to speak. The priest asked me what name he should give her. "Mary," I told him.'

We had discussed names a thousand times. I had wanted Colin for a boy or Mary for a girl, in honour of Our Lady.

'The priest turned to leave. Stricken with grief, I staggered after him, but he told me to remain with you.'

I stretched out my hand and gripped his. *All this had happened within such a short time, and I had not been there to share his sorrows.*

Chapter 2

That which does not kill makes us stronger, **Nietzsche**

ON THE MORNING I WAS discharged from hospital, slivers of sunlight streamed through the chinks in the vertical blinds. Birds sang outside my window. Colin signed the necessary papers before leading me to the car.

The sight of our lovely red brick ranch-style home with its red and yellow tiles filled me with pride at Colin's achievement. When he helped me out of the car, he swept me off my feet and carried me across the threshold. I felt like a bride entering her new home. During the three months I had been in hospital, Colin had painted the walls. We had discussed the colours previously and had chosen sky blue for the toilet, bathroom and the three bedrooms. Pale green for the kitchen. The lounge and dining rooms had multicoloured walls, which was in vogue at the time. One wall was hot pink, the others, daffodil yellow, sky blue and pale green. However, we had defied the fashion of shag-carpets, and chosen a pure wool Axminster because it was long-lasting, and we loved the classical design of red and gold with a touch of black. How delighted I was as Colin led me from room to room.

'I bought some second-hand furniture,' he said. 'That will have to do for the time being.'

'I love the house. The one thing missing is our baby.'

Colin placed an arm around me. 'As soon as you are stronger…'

We visited Dr Goulston at his surgery for more x-rays. 'You have three fractured ribs—the result of your fall in hospital. The stretching you did has set your ribs correctly. You're fortunate they did not puncture your lungs and cause them to collapse. A few scars remain but it is nothing to worry about.' He spoke slowly to emphasise the importance of his words. 'You are lucky to be alive. Your liver had dwindled to the size of a golf ball and was being consumed by your anti-bodies. It will grow back in time, but not have the same shape as previously.'

The doctor looked at Colin. 'The penicillin resulted in a massive allergic reaction. Your wife owes her life to the intern who acted so promptly by sending for me straight away. It may be too dangerous for her to conceive again.' He hesitated. 'Besides, your wife is not a young woman.'

Dark clouds enveloped me. I realised the doctor was looking at Colin, to emphasise the risk of my falling pregnant. My youthful desires had been fulfilled when I found love, but now my dreams of having a family were shattered.

Colin, on the other hand, appeared to accept the tragedy. A philosopher who bowed to the calamities of life, he concealed his misery, and held my frail body in his embrace. Perhaps he was hoping to infuse some of his strength into me.

We remained silent during the drive home, but when we arrived back, I burst out, 'Why didn't our General Practitioner refer me to an obstetrician when things got out of hand?'

Colin nodded. 'We should have insisted on one from the start, but he told us it was not necessary.'

'It's true I'm in my mid-thirties, but Mum had a child at 48. Why can't we have another child? I am never going back to *that* GP. It's all his fault. If it were not for him, we wouldn't have lost Mary.'

'But I'm sure he meant well. My family has been going to him ever since we moved to the ACT.'

I fumed. 'He should have known that the rash had been caused by the penicillin. He has been negligent.'

'It's too late to do anything about it now. We can't turn back the clock.' That was one of Colin's favourite expressions, but I felt that the doctor should be punished for his negligence. *Had he phoned the hospital and informed them of the penicillin injection, the resident doctor may have been able to do something about it without delay. Because of the GP we will now have to re-build our lives from the rubble of lost hopes.*

But in those days, doctors were trusted—regarded as demigods who knew everything about medicine.

In Buddhist culture, people are taught to revere God, the clergy, doctors and teachers. I was born in Burma, and even though I am a Eurasian and a Christian, their culture had rubbed off on me. I gave in to Colin, and never even considered suing the GP for his negligence. Yet for a long I distrusted doctors.

The following day, when Colin returned from work, he gave me a pair of runners. 'You'll need a comfortable pair of shoes when you start walking again.'

I looked at them in surprise and giggled because it was an effort to even walk from room to room. Then it dawned on me. He was hinting I should try walking again. 'Thank you, darling.' I hugged him with all my strength.

Determined not to be a burden, I concentrated on getting back to normal. I started with a few steps at a time while he was at work but had to pause for breath at the slightest incline. The first day I went as far as the neighbour's house, swaying slightly from the exertion.

On his return from work, I greeted Colin with a broad smile. 'I walked to the neighbour's house.' I must have sounded as excited as a child with a new toy.

The next evening, I said, 'I went as far as two houses.'

By the end of the week, I had walked past five houses. Delighted, Colin took me for short walks at weekends, increasing the distance each time.

When Colin considered me fit enough to know the truth, he told me everything that had occurred during my periods of swimming in and out of delirium. Mary had lived for three days. The priest had given him the name of a Funeral Director and he had arranged matters with him. In numbed abstraction, he went to our baby's burial—a funeral heralded by perfect spring weather.

In my mind, I saw the sun spread its warmth and feathery sprays of delicate green breaking forth, but the earth, bursting with new life, held our baby, still and silent, within its womb.

'The brightness of the sun had struck me like a spear,' Colin continued, 'and lost in a cruel vacuum, I brooded by the graveside. Torn with sorrow, I asked myself, *Will I lose my wife too? Whatever happens, life will never be the same again.*

'That evening, I drove home in a daze. No sooner had I unlocked the door, than the phone rang. I rushed to the telephone, thinking the hospital had rung. A voice said, "I wish to speak to Hazel Barker. She attended our Antenatal class once and didn't turn up for the next session. One of our pillows is missing. We'd like it back."'

Colin clenched his fists. 'My first impulse was to slam the receiver down without answering. My second, to let out such a roar of anger as to deafen the person at the other end, but I did neither. "My wife is in hospital and unable to attend further classes," I said, "She did not take your pillow." My chest heaving with rage, I put the phone down and stumbled out to the letterbox. Apart from the usual bills, I found an official-looking envelope and tore it open. *What now?* I scanned the page. It was a letter from Perth, telling me that, as you had sponsored your mother, May White, to Australia, you were responsible for her. It went on to say that Mrs White, who was currently teaching at a private school in Perth, had applied for a pension. Then it ended with, "The onus is on you, *not* the government to provide for her." I scrunched the letter. Too distraught at the time, I could only think of our lost child and our uncertain future. I flung the crumpled ball into the waste-paper basket and heated a can of soup for dinner.'

I stared aghast. *Poor Colin! Poor Mum!* 'Don't worry, darling. Mum knows I've been too ill to do anything about it right now.'

At the end of the financial year, we claimed our baby's funeral expenses, but it was rejected on the grounds we did not ever have a child. Angry and astounded, we produced Mary's death certificate. It took Colin several traumatic sessions and gruelling questions before the Taxation Office granted our claim.

August turned to October, and the skeletons of trees burst into bud. The daffodils Colin had planted peeped out shyly to greet the warm sunshine. Slowly, my strength returned.

Colin and I discussed the prospect of another pregnancy, and wondered what would have been the result of our baby's brain haemorrhage?

'Would Mary have suffered brain damage from the bleeding?' I asked him.

'Perhaps...'

'Our baby could have been like my brother, Herman. He was born with infantile paralysis and could not talk or feed himself. He often let out a piercing heart-rending cry, and we never knew how to relieve his pain. His entire life was miserable. God has spared Mary so much suffering.'

Colin folded me in his arms. 'She's now an angel in heaven. I'd rather have you than another child. I love you too much to risk losing you.' His voice sounded thick and hoarse.

We visited our baby's grave and sobs tore my chest as I wept for the first time. Colin clasped me in his arms and joined his tears to mine.

'Would you have re-married if I'd died?' I asked, waiting breathless for his reply.

He lowered his eyes. 'I'd have become a priest.'

I threw my arms around him. 'Your words touch me to the core. My heart swells with love. It's nearly bursting.'

Losing Mary did not put out the fire of Colin's enthusiasm. On completion of our new home, he turned his attention to building a rockery and birdbath in the garden. We probed the soil with our fingers, planting bulbs and seedlings.

In spring, on the anniversary of Mary's death, the cherry blossoms burst into bloom. I breathed in their sweet perfume. Sunshine glanced off leaves with a burst of colour from marigolds, hydrangeas, roses, rosemary and lavender. Daffodils reflected the golden sunlight and flooded our hearts with peace.

On winter days, I basked in the sun but kept indoors when the cold winds blew from the Snowy Mountains. Colin and I knew peace—a sense of tranquil happiness pervaded our lives. Our love for each other grew, but the sense of fulfillment eluded me.

One day, Colin took me to Bob Lucy, a natural therapist. After a course of vitamins and minerals, my health improved, and I felt strong enough to go for longer walks. On Sundays, we hiked in the Snowy Mountains or Brindabella, west of Canberra. Sometimes, an echidna, seeing us approach, would roll into a ball or dig into the soil with its claws to try to burrow out of sight. Once, we paused to gaze at a family of the little creatures ambling across our path. The young echidnas reminded me of our baby. We had planned to buy a papoose-carrier so we could take her for walks with us. A sudden pang of sorrow shot through my heart, while I prayed for strength to bear my cross.

The bushwalks grew longer and strengthened my feeble muscles. Within a year, I was hiking up to ten kilometres in a day. Losing our baby left a wound that healed over time but left a scar. We learned from our loss and resigned ourselves to God's will. Grief is like a shadow, but we tried not let it darken our lives.

Fourteen months after I had taken leave to have our baby, I returned to work in the Department of Customs and Excise. My friends, Jenny and John, greeted me with joy. They had been married during my absence, and were now just back at work, too. I took pride in the fact I had acted as cupid and whispered to John that Jenny was very much in love with him, so he should not play with her feelings but tell her what his intentions were. It had prompted him to propose to her.

I must have seemed like a ghost returning to haunt my workplace, because I was now as thin as a rake. My colleagues kindly refrained from offering their sympathies. I was glad—because I would probably have burst into tears. My body had been ravaged, but my mind was still clear. Although I was happy in the Public Service and had a good salary, I still longed for a teaching position. Before my marriage, I had loved the pupils in Perth, the shorter working hours and the longer holidays, so I hoped a position at St. Pat's, Braddon, would soon be available. I felt a degree in education would improve my chances of securing a teaching job. Another reason I wanted to further my studies was to prove to myself my illness had not affected my cognitive function. I made inquiries about further study now I had completed my BA and discovered that External Studies suited me. I discussed the matter with Colin, and we decided it would be possible to do this, but only if I was certain of getting a teaching position in the new academic year.

A few months later, the principal of St Pat's sent me a letter requesting an interview, as she needed a teacher for the following year. The interview was successful. Perhaps she was swayed by the fact that I contemplated enrolling for a Diploma in Teaching as an off-campus student.

I enrolled straight away but continued working in the Public Service until the first week of January when schools reopened after the long summer break.

Chapter 3

Canberra, 1973–1974

WE BOUGHT OURSELVES A TELEVISION set for Christmas. One day, while watching a travel documentary, Colin said, 'Why don't we go for a holiday?'

I had been sitting at his feet on our red Axminster carpet. I jumped up and hugged him. 'How exciting!'

In January, we flew to the north island of New Zealand. Wai-O-Tapu Wonderland with its green and yellow sands, thermal pools and vents thrilled us. At the hot springs in Rotorua the Lady Knox Geyser spewed tons of water and vapour.

We booked a flight to get a bird's eye view of the geysers. The pilot had flown a Spitfire during the London Blitz and asked, 'Would you like to experience some *real* flying?'

We nodded, not fully realising what he intended.

To our surprise, he made a low dive. Then he climbed and turned and dived again. My heart leapt to my throat. I think I left my stomach behind. We flew over the geyser and watched the thick lava bubble erupt, propelling jets of steam into the air. Water sprinkled the windows of our plane. I swallowed hard; my lips dry from the sheer thrill of flying so close to ground level.

Once again, he turned, and diving even lower, headed straight for a bridge. The pylons on either side of us grew closer. My eyes widened in horror and my hands tightened on the arms of my seat as I prayed for our safety. The wings of our plane seemed to touch the pylons. Once again, I left my stomach behind. We cleared the bridge by millimetres and gained height. I could scarcely believe we had flown *under* the overpass.

After his display of aerobatics, the pilot landed the craft, his face wreathed in smiles.

The trip to New Zealand refreshed our spirits and whetted our appetite for more travel both in Australia and overseas. Like a delicious dish of food, we craved more.

I commenced teaching at St Pat's soon after our return. By then, Mum was on a pension and Social Services were no longer hounding us for her financial support.

At St Pat's, I often met Father O'Shea, the priest who had said the Nuptial Mass when we married at the little church of St Xavier in February 1971. He offered his condolences when he heard of the loss of our baby. He recommended joining Teams of Our Lady.

'What do they do?' I asked.

'They meet monthly to reflect on the Gospel and share their spiritual journey.'

'How will that help us, Father?'

'It is an International Catholic Association of married couples to implant the essential values of a Christian marriage. It will enrich your marriage. You will learn a lot from each other and grow in trust and friendship. It's like having a second family.'

I looked at Colin, but he remained silent.

'At the moment, I am too busy with my new job, but we certainly will look into it, Father.'

'God bless you both. You may want to try it someday.'

Father Flack, our parish priest, paid particular attention to us, perhaps because Father O'Shea had asked him to keep a watchful eye. He would frequently drop in for a chat. One day he suggested,

'Why not adopt a child? There are so many orphans who are waiting for a good home.'

Colin and I were not too keen, but we promised to consider his advice. However, nothing came of it. Not long after, Father Flack had a heart attack, was hospitalised, and visitors were prohibited. When he recovered, he was posted to a quiet parish in the countryside. We missed him and sorely regretted his departure.

I made many friends at St. Pat's, especially in the English and History departments, as well as colleagues in the mathematics department, as I also taught that subject.

I had a particular friend, Patsy Sheales, whose husband's work involved research on native animals. Patsy taught Home Economics and was an excellent cook. She often invited us over for dinner. One day, she brought up the subject of Marriage Encounter.

'You should try Marriage Encounter. It's a weekend getaway for couples to recharge their relationship batteries.'

'But our marriage is perfect,' I said. 'Isn't that only for couples whose marriages are on the rocks?'

'It's meant to enrich your marriage. Not to mend it. That's for a marriage counsellor. Terry and I have had a Marriage Encounter weekend. It's marvellous.' Patsy was so persuasive that we agreed to try it.

Marriage Encounter Weekends are a time away from all distractions. A Team of three married couples and a priest made a series of presentations. After each session, we examined ourselves, our behaviours, attitudes, and our relationship with our each other and with God. We were given time on our own and asked to write about things that annoyed us about our partner. These letters were private and no one else saw them except our partners.

It helped couples connect in healthy, constructive ways to deepen their intimacy. At the end of each session, Colin and I exchanged letters. I still treasure them, along with the ones he wrote before our marriage. One letter in particular led us to discover that we each did what we thought the other wanted. At times, it that made us do the things neither of us desired.

I can never forget one couple who stood apart at the beginning, while the rest of us held hands with our partners. After the first session, the estranged pair moved closer, and by the end of the Marriage Encounter weekend, they too were holding hands.

To our surprise, the Marriage Encounter weekend helped Colin and I communicate even better than previously. It deepened our relationship and we learnt to be more open with each other. Being honest about what we really wanted, we could make the right decisions. From Marriage Encounter, we learned to speak frankly to each other, and thus avoid mistakes. I am ever grateful to my friend Patsy for pointing us in the right direction.

My studies entailed attendance at lectures in New England during school vacations. Colin dropped me off at the airport and I flew up to Armidale where I resided on campus at Earle Page College.

Mature green trees in the university grounds extended their arms in greeting when the pick-up bus drove into the campus. As it was at the end of term, most of the 300 students had returned home for the holidays, so that gave me a lot of time to do my research in the library. I attended lectures in psychology and behavioural studies, and had my meals in the large dining room, which held a grand piano. In between lectures, research and meals, I walked daily in the beautiful grounds and enjoyed the pristine air of the New England highlands.

The two weeks away from Colin during the spring and autumn holidays made our partings seem like an eternity.

Colin said, 'I'd been worried for you at first, but, recalling your long flight from Burma to Australia all alone in 1967, I relaxed.'

We joined the Orienteering Association and the National Parks Organisation. At instruction sessions, we were given a map showing forests, water courses, clearings, trails and roads, ditches, fences and powerlines, buildings, boulders, and other terrain features. We had to use a compass to find our way via control points with red and white markers that looked like paper lanterns. We had to stamp our map at each marker.

Names were called at intervals, so each participant set out separately. The one who completed their course first was the winner. Colin enjoyed competing with men of his age group. He always completed long before me, even though I ran with the beginners.

One Sunday, I lost my way and began to panic, even though I knew the organisers would never leave until all competitors had checked in. Perspiration poured out of my body. My eyes darted from side to side, looking for clues.

Time and time again, I called out, 'Colin. I'm lost.'

My weak and trembling voice failed to reach anyone. Kookaburras cackled. Leaves rustled but no answer came. Fear clutched my heart. I saw a red and white orienteering sign beaming in the distance. Tied to a tree among the scrub, it was like a beacon to a ship in a storm. Thinking it was the control point I was looking for, I ran through the bush, scratching my face and arms on thorny bushes. To my dismay, the number on the marker was not on my beginner's map. I must have strayed and come across one of the more advanced competitors' markers. I stumbled back. My mouth was dry. My heart thudded and my eyes dimmed with tears. I staggered on. *If I keep on the track, Colin will find me. It is so much easier to see a person on a track than within the scrub.*

I kept going, knowing my knight-in-shining-armour would come to save me as he always did. After several hours, he found me scratched and dishevelled. I staggered and threw myself, crying, into his arms. Holding me close, Colin stroked my hair.

Later that day, he related what he had done. 'Most of the others from your group had already drifted in, so I was worried. I located a map of the beginner's course and scoured the forest. You were not on the route, so I guessed you must have wandered off. I blamed myself for letting you go on your own. You know how to use a map and compass, but I don't think you are well enough.' He gazed at me for a long moment. 'In future, we'll give up orienteering and only go bushwalking.'

'No. Orienteering gives you a chance to compete with others. Besides, I slow you down too much when bushwalking. I can't keep up.'

He smiled and gave me a hug. 'You have an indomitable spirit. Soon you'll be doing twenty kilometres a day and we can reconsider coming back to orienteering.'

Colin sacrificed orienteering for me, so I tried my hardest to grow strong again by not giving in to weariness. I promised myself I would never be a burden to him. I recalled the times I had a cough as a child during the war, and Mum used to rub my chest with camphor oil to ease my breathing. My coughing had stopped when hostilities ceased, and our diet improved. *Surely, I'll get over this too.*

The bushwalks grew longer in proportion to my strength, but my cough persisted despite vitamins and minerals as well as an occasional puff of Ventolin. Exercise improved my lungs, yet my coughing came and went with the seasons. It seemed to grow worse every spring and at the end of each school term.

'Perhaps the stress of your job makes your cough worse,' Colin said. 'You always get better after a weekend at the coast. At Eden.'

'Maybe it's the fresh air,' I said.

We frequently spent weekends at Eden on the southern coast of New South Wales. Colin glanced at the holiday homes that fringed the coastline from Bateman's Bay to Eden, then northwards to Sydney and beyond. 'We'll build a holiday home like other Canberrans someday.'

I loved the countryside and, as I saw more and more of the bush, I too fell in love with the Australian landscape.

During our long drives, we listened to John Denver's *Take Me Home, Country Roads* and *Rocky Mountain High*. We enjoyed songs like *He Ain't Heavy*, *Mr Bojangles*, *Tie a Yellow Ribbon* and *Paper Roses*. Although sad, the lyrics acclaimed nature and love. We cherished both. How fresh the world seemed each morning! Cat Stevens' *Morning Has Broken* remained the top hit of the day. The words were apt too.

We sometimes drove to Brindabella, or Blundell's Flat in the northwestern corner of the ACT and only about 27 km from home. It is encircled by hills and mountain ranges covered by native forest, though some areas were planted with Pinus Radiata. We particularly loved the arboreta of conifers and poplars with their visual diversity. Whenever we spent the day there, we would pick water cress from the clear streams and add them to our salad.

Our days were filled with love and joy. Only two years previously, the specialist had told us that, even if I lived through the crisis, I would be an invalid for the rest of my life. Yet by the grace of God, our tears had washed away our sorrow, and I had recovered my health.

The bushwalks and orienteering were welcome distractions to help us ease the loss of our baby. The thought of her death had tolled in the belfry of my mind, but now I felt as though a spring had been released within me. Our faith in the Lord had pulled us through such a dark time in our lives. His healing grace gave us the resilience to rise above our sorrow, and our love for each other had burgeoned over the years.

    We thanked the Lord for restoring my health. My recovery had been a miracle.

Chapter 4

My Family

MY ELDER BROTHER, BERTIE, migrated to Australia in 1973. Mum had been onto him to join us, and I was delighted that all my family was now in the same country.

My sister Rose had written words of sympathy to us soon after Mary died. We always communicated with each other even if only indirectly through Mum's letters. My two brothers rarely wrote. The men of our family suppressed their emotions and neither had sent condolences. Our early upbringing had taught us to conceal our innermost feelings, so their apparent lack of sympathy did not bother me.

However, Bertie wrote saying he would be flying over from Perth. I had not seen him in 14 years when he had visited me in Lashio prior to leaving Burma for the UK.

I was shocked at his appearance. I had expected to see a good-looking young man. Instead he was chubby, with a protruding stomach and a receding hairline. But he was still my brother. We hugged and I introduced him to Colin, brought out some refreshments, and sank down on a comfortable armchair.

It took me a while to adjust. As we spoke, the veil lifted, and I realised only Bertie's looks had changed. His mannerisms were the same. His voice was the same: melodious and clear.

Bertie recalled his life since we last met. 'After I said goodbye to Mum, Rose and Winston in Mandalay, I drove down to Rangoon. Our cousins greeted me with open arms, and I enjoyed many happy weekends with aunty and uncle. Dad had never showed me any affection but, wishing to make peace with him before leaving, I obtained his address from aunty.'

I leaned forward, recalling the long sepulchral silences interspersed by harsh words and blows from father.

'I had imagined the meeting with dad a thousand times,' Bertie went on. 'The quick recognition, the warm embrace and tears. Wondering how everything would turn out, I stretched out my hand, half-expecting it to be ignored.'

I drew a deep breath, reluctant to interrupt my brother.

'Trembling, Dad took my hand and offered me a seat,' Bertie continued. 'He spoke of the past without any sign of anger or hatred. Encouraged by this, I asked him why he had retired from his position at the High Court so soon after we'd left. He said he could no longer bear the gossip among his colleagues and imagined them laughing behind his back because his family had deserted him. He'd retired, a broken man.'

A flush of joy burned my face to know my father had finally received what he deserved.

'Dad told me that he drank more and more to forget his humiliation, but alcohol only kept the past fresh in his mind,' Bertie went on. 'He said he'd stumbled home drunk every evening. At times, he did not even make it back but collapsed on the ground or rolled into the gutter. When some form of sense returned with daylight, he would stagger home to start the day's cycle all over again. It hurt me to see him fallen so low. I invited him for a drive to our old haunts.'

I listened, amazed that suffering had humbled our dominating and brutal father. I wished Colin and I could visit Burma and see all the old familiar places of my childhood days together—Monkey Point, the Kokine Lakes, the Royal Lakes.

I glanced at Colin, but his eyes were fixed on Bertie.

'When we returned from the drive, Dad asked, "Who taught you how to drive?" Glad to let him know he had unwittingly been my teacher, I told him I used to watch him when I was a child, so I passed my driving test without any instructions.'

I nodded, realising that Bertie had always craved his father's love.

'I held Dad close before leaving. He returned my embrace and I departed in peace.' Bertie's voice choked as he spoke.

Filled with admiration at my brother's forgiving nature, I said, 'That was so noble of you. I still can't forgive him.'

I thought he would rebuke me, but he ignored me and continued, 'Dad's de facto bore him two children. They're both girls...'

So now I have two half-sisters. But they are his children and not Mum's. No sense of kinship rose within me. For the first time in my life, I realised how deeply the hatred of my father's behaviour had embedded itself into my soul. I recalled how I had struggled to forgive him during my years as a novice. Bertie had such a forgiving nature. *Why can't I be like him? But I had been bitterly wronged, and I clung to my desire for revenge. Only hell itself would be enough punishment for him.*

'It took weeks before all the red tape was completed, and I could leave for London.' Bertie's voice took on a happier note. 'When my ship steamed away from port the next day, I thought of the sea voyage with Dad and Mum, Rupert, June and you when we took the Toy train up to Darjeeling. Do you remember?' He paused to sip his coffee. The corners of his eyes moistened as other memories intruded. 'Rupert, June, Herman and Trevor are all buried in Burmese soil. But Mum, Rose and Winston and you were still living in a country torn by civil war. I wanted to prepare a place for you all.'

'And you have, too,' I said. 'You went to Australia House to search for our grandfather's birth certificate so that we could obtain residence in the UK, and you found a situation for each of us in the UK.'

A lump stuck in my throat, choking me, as my thoughts swung to my dead siblings. *June had died during the war and Rupert had passed away soon after hostilities ended. Herman faded away later. Then little Trevor.* I turned from Bertie to Colin for comfort.

He gave me a hug. Somehow, Colin always seemed able to read my thoughts. Children from large families could appreciate the joys of having siblings, yet Colin, who had no brother and only one sister, understood how I felt for my family.

Just as Bertie used to relate his boyhood adventures, he settled into a story-telling mode. 'Mum had written asking her old school friend to give me a home until I found work. I stayed with her until I enrolled as a student nurse at Longrove Hospital in Surrey. As soon as I stepped into the hospital mortuary, memories of my studies at medical college in Rangoon flashed through my mind. My hands used to stink after dissecting body parts. The cadaver's skin looked like leather and an acrid smell saturated the room. The smell made me think of Rupert and that Japanese soldier's skull he kept in his bedroom.'

I remembered the skull with its grinning teeth and hollow eye sockets. And the stench. After the re-capture of Mandalay by Allied troops during World War II, we had found a dead Japanese officer laid out on a bed. Rupert had chopped off his head but was unable to scrape off all the dead flesh and skin from the skull, so bits had hung on, making it stink. During the war years, Death was our neighbour but never a friend. The Angel of Death always hovered above. We could almost hear its wings beating.

'I moved into the nurses' quarters. It increased my loneliness,' Bertie continued. 'The gardens in Surrey are beautiful. Houses are decorated with miniature rabbits, dolls, or teddy bears but no dogs dig for bones and no children play in the gardens. Not when I was there, anyway. In spite of my loneliness, I had settled in by the time spring arrived. I loved feeding the thrushes and blackbirds with crumbs from the table. How they shrieked and scolded. In summer, I bought an eight foot-long-boat and rowed up and down the Thames. Sometimes, I would stop to feed the ducks or chat with the lockkeeper. Wish you had been there. You'd have enjoyed yourself...'

'How delightful! I would have loved to have been there too. But in a convent, all I wanted was to dedicate my life to God.'

Bertie nodded. 'It snowed during my first year in England, turning Box Hill, a favourite spot with tobogganers, into a fairyland. Everything looked fresh and new. I adored the English winters and the cold, crisp air. I built a toboggan.'

Colin coughed. 'We've been to the Snowy Mountains and enjoyed ourselves in the snow, too. I know exactly how you felt.'

Bertie acknowledged Colin's comment with a smile. 'I travelled all over the country with my tent and motorcycle. To Devon and Cornwall and the beautiful Lake District.'

Colin was listening intently. He had been born in Nottingham but had left when his parents emigrated to Australia. *It will be wonderful to visit England with Colin,* I thought.

Bertie went on reminiscing. 'In North Wales, I once stopped to ask permission to camp on a farmer's property. After pitching my tent, I returned to the farmhouse for some eggs. When the farmer's wife saw me, she called out to her husband. "Thomas, there's a foreigner to see you." Thomas chided his wife. "The stranger is not to be referred to as a foreigner, but by his name." I immediately felt at home.'

Bertie spoke to us about this incident several times in the ensuing years, and we knew he had been deeply touched by the words of the friendly Welshman. I had been more fortunate in Australia, as the people in Perth had been friendly to me right from the start.

In 1974, a few months after Bertie returned to Perth, my young brother Winston drove across the Nullarbor to Canberra. I was overjoyed to see him again. He had grown now and sported an athletic figure. How different he was from the teenager I had accompanied from Mandalay to the Rangoon airport when he, too, had left for the UK.

'I drove to Sydney and went to the notorious King's Cross.' Unlike Bertie, he did not speak much of his time in the UK or Perth.

I was working as a teacher and could not spend time with him except after school. To my disappointment, he did not stay with us long enough.

After Winston's departure, Colin said, 'I've never known the joys of a large family, but your sufferings as children and teenagers must have helped bond your family.'

I hugged him. He was always so understanding. As children, my siblings had developed a strong bond and our joys had multiplied because we always rejoiced when something good happened to one of us. I recalled the pride I had felt when my sister June had been called up by the principal to receive her prize for being top of the class, and when either June or Rose performed at school concerts, or my brothers did something brave. I remembered my joy when young Winston earned his black belt in karate and when all my family had joined me in Australia.

My heart had been torn in two when my father had belted my brothers or beaten Mum, but our sorrows had been lightened because we shared each other's burdens. I knew that they, in turn, had sympathised with me when my father slapped my face whenever it took his fancy.

Chapter 5

Canberra, 1975–1983

WHEN SUMMER GAVE WAY TO autumn, we bought a Heron—a twelve-foot boat with a jib and mainsail. At weekends, Colin showed off his skills, throwing back his head in exultation as the sails obeyed his every command. I loved watching him manoeuvre the boat and enjoyed the thrill of skimming through the water and the soft kiss of the breeze as it tousled my hair. Ripples ran against our bows like the sound of a lute among the reeds. Boats drifted on the water like tiny moths, wings caught in a web of sunshine.

I recalled my days in Burma when we went swimming in the Kokine Lakes on Sundays, and I would watch couples in their yachts and long for the day I too would go sailing with a handsome young man. Now, God had granted me my wish.

One Sunday, strong winds whipped up the water, but we ignored the warning signs, strapped on our lifejackets and set sail. Colin had been a Sea Cadet and risen to Leading Seaman in Portland. As a young boy, he had been out with the fishing fleet. 'If the boat capsizes, remember to jump off on the side opposite the rigging,' he reminded me.

'But it won't overturn, will it?' I remembered the three balls outside the Canberra Yacht Club, warning of wild weather.

He smiled, obviously confident in his own prowess. Filled with the spirit of fun and adventure, we sped off. The Heron sliced through heaving water. I squealed with delight. Colin blew a kiss, threw back his shoulders and thrust out his chest. It was delightful to see him pitting his strength against the unleashed fury of the gale. The boat skimmed along, lithe and graceful as a swan.

A sudden gust caught us. Colin wrestled with the ropes. I held my breath. *Wish I could help him.* I remained glued to my seat. The wind increased in velocity and the boat tipped over, throwing us overboard.

I sank into the depths of the lake; my lungs about to burst. *I can't breathe much longer. Soon, I'll black out. I'll drown.* I gave a desperate kick and popped up like a cork from a champagne bottle.

Colin was in the water some distance away, his head turning as he scanned the lake for me. 'Are you all right, darling?' he shouted. 'Swim for the boat.'

We swam to the Heron and rocked and heaved to set it upright. The sails, laden with water, made it too heavy for us. Eventually, we gave up and clung to the sides, looking everywhere for help. But others had been more cautious and sailed close to the shore, too far off to see us.

I hung on to the side of the Heron, hair drenched, teeth chattering.

The sun was about to set and it was becoming unbearably cold. We could not remain hanging on to the boat for a whole night, so once again, we tried to right it. All to no avail.

My feet were numb. The coldness crept upwards. Our situation was desperate. Too far off to attempt swimming to shore, all we could do was to hang on and pray for deliverance.

I lost track of time… A humming sound jolted me back to consciousness. I opened my eyes. A motorboat with *River Police* marked clearly on its sides was puttering towards us.

'Would you like a tow?'

'Yes please,' we sang out in unison.

Immediately, I sent up a silent prayer of thanksgiving. Within minutes, we stood shivering on the bank. We had no change of clothing in the car, so Colin turned the heater on high and we drove home, teeth chattering. A hot shower and a warm bed with an electric blanket soon thawed our frozen bodies.

That night in bed, Colin said, 'I shouldn't have taken you out in such unpredictable conditions. When you were clinging to the boat, you looked dazed. Your lips were blue with the cold, but I saw them moving in silent prayer, so I joined you.'

'Why didn't you jump off the side? I was so worried!'

A flush rose to Colin's face. 'It happened so suddenly, and I had no time to jump. I was entangled in the rigging down below and had to extricate myself. My eyes darted frantically around, looking for you. The ropes slid off my legs after one final kick, and a few upward strokes brought me to the surface.'

We fell asleep in each other's arms.

The next morning, Colin washed the Heron and stored it in the garage. Winter was fast approaching, the boating season nearly over. Humbled but wiser for our experience, we discussed the accident.

'We'll stick to gardening and bushwalking, but before we sell her, we must take the Heron out once more or the fear of water will remain with you,' Colin said. 'I don't want you to live in dread of sailing.'

The experience had shaken me, but I did not want Colin to give up sailing. 'But you love the water. Can't we bushwalk and sail on alternate weekends?'

'Sailing in the lake is not like sailing in the sea.'

'What's the difference? I thought it would be easier as the waves are smaller.'

'In ocean sailing, the waves are bigger, but the wind does not come in gusts like it does in Burley Griffin.'

'But why?'

'Because the terrain channels the wind to blow in gusts. In blue water where the waves are bigger, we spend a lot more time learning to handle the large waves and manage the boat when it rolls in swells. We also have to excel in navigating, whereas lake sailors concentrate on tacking and are expert at it.'

All this sounded rather mysterious, but I came to the conclusion Colin was interested in sailing in the ocean, not on a lake.

Once the cherry blossoms announced the arrival of spring, we took the boat down to Lake Burley Griffin. Peaceful and still, the water shimmered with reflected sunlight. Gentle waves lapped the sides of the Heron. The air was soporific, benign. Our hearts ached with the thought of giving up our treasure, but we knew we were doing the right thing. We were destined for the land. We were bushwalkers, not boaties.

The next day, we put an advertisement in the papers and sold our yacht to the first inquirer.

We now went camping during weekends. At Mt Kosciusko, I marvelled at the rugged peaks and the white slopes. At Perisher Valley in the Snowy Mountains National Park, Colin hired a toboggan and sat in front. We sped down the slopes. My cheeks tingled. I hung on to the sides in sheer delight as everything whizzed past.

We got off at the bottom, laughing and dusting the snow off our clothes. 'I first saw snow on the Himalayas at the age of three when we went on a holiday to Darjeeling,' I told Colin, 'but the snow-covered mountains were so far away.'

Colin had had skiing lessons, but all this was new to me. 'In Burma I often saw photos of Lifeguards on Bondi Beach, and kangaroos and koalas running wild in the bush, so I always thought of Australia as a land of beaches, eucalyptus trees, kangaroos and koalas. I never guessed I'd see snow.'

'Just seeing your face light up with joy makes me feel ten feet tall,' Colin said.

Summer in the Snowy Mountains was a sensation. At times, we camped at Kiandra. Gold had been discovered there in 1859, and by March 1860, the population had reached more than 10,000 people of several nationalities. By 1861, gold ran out and the prospectors moved to Lambing Flat. The population then dropped to 250. Now all that remains is an old house, and the Court House.

We walked the Heritage Trail, which shows photos of the former town. I loved the carpet of many-hued Russel lupins planted by the pioneers. I was so impressed that, when teaching the gold rushes to my Year Nine class, I took them there for a two-day excursion. We had a wonderful time, but my students kept me awake all night running along the corridors and visiting each other.

The Head of the History Department objected to the girls going on an excursion without another teacher, so my friend, Sally Brideoake, and I planned to combine our classes for a trip to Tasmania the following year. Our plans came to nothing, however, as Sally went on maternity leave.

During school holidays, Colin and I went further afield—Kangaroo Valley, Moss Vale, the Blue Mountains, and the Bunya Mountains—pitching our tents in caravan parks and cooking our meals on a camp stove.

'I'll show you how to make tea in a billy can,' Colin said, 'and how to roast potatoes in a campfire.'

Eager to learn, I too, grew to love camping. Our two favourite haunts were Eden and the Snowy Mountains.

Despite my happiness, I never forgot my family. I often thought of Mum's visit at the hospital and hoped we could meet under happier circumstances.

Mum had taught me the basic steps of the waltz and, because I adored it, Colin and I enrolled in dance lessons. At times, I tended to lead as Colin had never danced before, and I knew the steps. Much as Colin loved me, he resented being led. He would stand still and refuse to budge.

'The lady has to *follow*, not *lead*,' the instructor kept reminding me.

I would blush and promise not to do it again.

I loved sliding across the waxed floor. Dance for me is an intense communion between mind and body. The waltz linked our bodies and allowed us to move in harmony. Waltzing soothed my senses while it stimulated my passion for Colin. The world melted away and I would lose myself in his sure-handed and supportive grip. Colin too adored waltzing, but he preferred rocking and rolling to Golden Oldies like Bill Haley's *Rock Around the Clock* and tunes by the Beatles. We danced at socials, entered a competition for beginners, and even won the first prize for Rock and Roll.

Years later, we moved to the Redlands in Queensland and met the Bartells, a couple from Burma. Lt-Colonel Bartells persuaded us to join the RSL and we danced at the club whenever they had a big band. We also went to the Sea Gulls Club at Tweed Heads with our friends Jim and Barbara Phillips.

I loved the dark blue ceiling studded with twinkling lights. It was like dancing beneath the stars. So romantic. At such times, I felt young and carefree. I had finally succeeded in burying my grief for the loss of our baby.

Chapter 6

1974–1976

AFTER COMPLETING MY STUDIES at New England, I enrolled in the Queensland Institute of Natural Science for a Diploma in Herbal Medicine and Naturopathy. When qualified, we set up a naturopathic clinic, and I saw my patients after school.

Colin often told me of his final years at High School. 'I wanted to join the British Navy but had been advised to further my education, but my parents withdrew me from school, and I missed the chance. Now, although I no longer wish to go to sea, I long to improve my prospects in life.'

He worked in the State Public Service Department of Building at the time and knew the government would reimburse the fees on completion of his degree, so he enrolled in a Bachelor in Town Planning course at the University of New England, taking two units—History and Geography.

Studies entailed lectures during the summer vacation. I always accompanied him to Armidale as I was on holiday. We drove through the old winding Putty Road to Penrith, passing forests of eucalyptus on either side. Two National Parks beckoned us, but we resisted the temptation to stop, flitting past farmlands at Muswellbrook, Scone and Tamworth.

The first year of Colin's studies passed without problems. Our studies did not interfere with our weekly walks, and added greater variety to our lives. In his second year, during one of our trips to Brindabella, we came across a heap of brumbies' droppings.

'That'll be great manure for our garden.' While bending over to collect the horse dung, an excruciating pain shot through Colin's back. He staggered to the car and collapsed onto the passenger seat. 'Feels like a vice is crushing my vertebrae.'

We had no analgesics with us, so I drove him to a doctor.

'Looks like a slipped disc. You need an operation.'

We had heard of many unsuccessful back operations where the patient could never walk again. So Colin kept putting it off, but the agony increased whenever he sat down. The pain prevented him from keeping pace with assignments, so he withdrew from the course. I thought of his frustrated hopes as a boy when his parents had withdrawn him from high school early, and I spent many sleepless nights worrying about him.

Fortunately, his back improved after months of treatment from a chiropractor. Our faith in natural healing escalated. Soon, Colin, too, became interested in Natural Medicine, so we both attended a course in Nutrition and Biochemistry in Sydney. Lectures on Saturdays were followed by practical sessions on Sundays. Although we normally stopped at caravan parks during holidays, we now stayed at a hotel—a luxurious experience. After lectures, we would visit places like the Rocks, Bondi Beach, the Sydney Harbour Bridge and Darling Harbour. We were too busy to brood over the baby or Colin's lost chances of higher education.

Overseas and interstate travel broadened our knowledge and widened our experience. In August 1974, during the spring vacation, we flew to Cairns, hired a car, and drove to the Atherton Tableland, Port Douglas and Cooktown. In Port Douglas, I tugged Colin's arm at the familiar sight of coconut palms. 'Look. Fresh coconuts. I haven't seen them *in situ* for ages. We had a coconut palm in our garden when I was a child.'

'I have never tasted a fresh coconut,' Colin said.

The palms waved in the breeze, and some coconuts lay around on the ground, so I picked one up and handed it to Colin. 'Just hack the top off and peel the husks. It will look like a head or skull with three eyes. Poke out one of the eyes and the drink pours out easily.'

Colin always carried a hunting knife during our walks. He made short work of opening the coconut, and we enjoyed a feast of the delicious white kernel and coconut juice.

That summer, we drove to Victoria and camped at Hall's Gap where koalas ambled across the road and visited our camp site. I loved watching them and longed to cuddle one. We hiked in the Grampians, then drove to Ballarat and Bendigo, visiting Sovereign Hill and Swan Hill where I learned more of life during the gold rushes as well as the early lifestyle of pioneers. I brought home several books and pamphlets for my Year 9 history class.

Back in Perth, Bertie had married Ann, his sweetheart of days gone by. Mum moved in with them and continued writing every week. Even though we were miles apart, our letters drew us close.

'God has answered my prayers and fulfilled all my wishes,' Mum wrote. 'My children have all married in church and Ann is expecting Bertie's child.'

I was delighted to know that Bertie, who loved children dearly, was to have a family of his own. I knew he would give his wife all the care she needed and use his knowledge of medicine to watch over her. Even though Bertie was older than me, Ann was younger. I hoped the baby would be strong and healthy.

I had not seen my mother since the loss of Mary, and I longed for her to visit. So in January 1975 we paid for her return plane fare from Perth to Brisbane.

The night before her arrival, I was so excited that sleep was as far from me as the stars in the sky. When we picked her up at the airport, I noticed Mum's hair had thinned and turned from light brown to silver. Yet she was a beautiful as ever. I held her tight. Her body felt frail, but her smile lit up her whole face.

In the mornings, when Colin left for work, I drove Mum to the pine forests and placed a blanket on the ground among the St. John's Wort. The sweet fragrance of the pines drifted to us as we talked of family matters.

'Rose is expecting her second child,' Mum said. 'What have you done with your baby's clothes?'

I turned my head to hide my tears. 'I've put them away, hoping to forget our sorrow.'

She took my hand and stroked it. 'Rose has given all her baby's things away. Her first delivery was so traumatic that she had not intended to have any more children. Why not give them to her?'

Back at home I packed the blue outfit I had knitted, as well as other baby items—the last physical link with our little angel. All my long-suppressed feelings broke open in a wild torrent of emotion as I handed them to Mum. 'Perhaps they'll be of use to Rose. I'll only brood over our loss.'

I thought we had got over it, but a scab had formed, covering the festering wound. Parting from my baby's clothes tore it off.

Mum kissed me and put them in her portmanteau. 'Ever since her caesarean, Rose won't go swimming because she says her tummy is too large.'

'Tell her to wear a swimsuit with a top that covers her stomach,' I said.

The next time we went shopping together, I bought Rose a pair of bathers with a high-waisted skirt, and asked Mum to give them to her.

My mother never failed to point me in the right direction or stir my conscience. Giving away Mary's things must have helped towards healing my wound, because since then, I stopped mourning at each anniversary of her death, and celebrated Mothers' Day by thinking of Mary as a cherub in Heaven.

Every evening, I would tell Colin how I spent the day with Mum. After dinner, we played records of the Golden Oldies. Mum joined in the singing, seeming to shed years off her age. On weekends, we showed her the sights. She particularly enjoyed the trips to Tidbinbilla Reserve. Her face would light up when she fed the kangaroos and emus. Little things pleased her, and my heart expanded to share our happiness.

'I will return to Perth at the end of the school holiday,' she said, after a couple of weeks.

'Why are you leaving so soon?' I asked.

'I'm so happy to see that you and Colin are devoted to each other, and I've enjoyed the peace and harmony at your place, but you will be busy when school re-opens. Besides, Rose and Ann will need me during their pregnancy.'

If only Mum had been with me during my pregnancy when I had no one to advise me.

Mum stayed for five glorious weeks. For the second time, I reluctantly let her leave. She placed her hand over mine. 'I've divided my money equally between Bertie, you, Rose and Winston, and I've asked your friend Gem Ballantyne to act as my executor.'

My heart shrivelled. I could not bear the thought of life without my mother. She had guided my infant steps and shaped my life. I clasped her frail body.

On the way to the airport, I tried my best to be cheerful. 'We'll visit you and the rest of the family once the Nullarbor is sealed.' My lashes were wet, and Mum's mouth twisted with suppressed emotion. I had seen this expression on her face so many times as a child when sorrow had wrung her heart, but I consoled myself with the thought we would visit her soon.

Despite my attempt at a smile, I had a sense of foreboding as she left. She had grown so thin and frail in the last eight years. Like an autumn leaf about to blow away in the wind.

We waited impatiently for the Department of Works to seal the final sections of the road across the Nullarbor, so we could have a family reunion in Perth.

That year in September, Winston married an Australian girl. Unfortunately, we had been unable to attend his wedding. I agonised over it, but we had already paid for Mum's return airfare earlier that year and were still paying off the house loan. Had we known of his wedding then, perhaps we would have waited for another eight months to see Mum and attend the wedding as well.

During the Christmas holidays of 1975, we grabbed the offer of a tour of the west coast of the United States and Mexico advertised at a heavily discounted rate. 'We can't miss this opportunity,' Colin said. 'This is not even as expensive as a flight to Perth. Domestic flights within Australia are far too much. We'll wait to drive over to Perth rather than fly, next year.'

'How true,' I said. 'The price includes a tour of the US west coast and Mexico. Even our plane fares.'

If we had been able to foresee the future, we would never have taken the tour. Yet the years ahead remained hidden, so we toured the US from December 19 to January 4. At Disneyland we re-lived our childhood fantasies. We marvelled at the filming secrets of Universal Studios in Los Angeles, walked down the most crooked street in San Francisco and tucked into fresh seafood at Fisherman's Wharf.

Our coach proceeded to Mexico City where we spent Christmas and New Year. The tour included a night at a bull ring. Many people regard bull fights as a cruel sport, and I wondered how I would feel after watching one. I had read D. H. Lawrence's account of a bull fight in *The Plumed Serpent* and recalled his description of the picadors' horses being gored. I shuddered. *But that book had been first published in 1926. Surely today, the country would have done away with such cruelty.*

The women were dressed in colourful clothes and the men in their Sunday best. Food and drink vendors thronged around. The seats were concrete, but the gradient was steep enough to have a good view of the arena.

'You have tickets for the best seats,' the guide said. 'I didn't get you ringside seats because a bull sometimes jumps the fence and causes havoc in the first row of spectators.'

My breath quickened at the sight of the huge crowd. Amidst fanfare, the matador entered the ring. He wore a silk jacket heavily embroidered in gold, and skin-tight trousers. His entire outfit sparkled in the sun. Banderilleros and picadors followed him, but left the arena before the bullpen gate opened.

Lance in hand, the matador met the charging bull with a series of dexterous manoeuvres of his red cape. Again and again the bull charged, throwing the whole of its 460 kg weight upon the cape. The applause was deafening.

The matador bowed, and his horse pranced out of the arena amid loud cheers. Then the picadors entered on horseback. Unlike bullfights of Lawrence's time, the picadors' horses were padded for protection with their legs covered by steel leg-armour. I sighed with relief to know the horses would not be hurt.

Armed with lances, the picadors wore felt hats and silver embroidered jackets. After many feints with their lances, they succeeded in piercing the bull in three places. Blood flowed from the wounds.

'Why do they torture the poor bull?' I asked Colin.

'To enrage it, so that it puts up a good show.'

A trumpet blew and the banderilleros advanced on foot, holding their brightly adorned barbed sticks. Although dressed like the matador, their suits were embroidered in silver, not gold. Once they had succeeded in piercing the bull's neck with the barbs, they retreated.

'What needless torture,' I whispered.

Colin sighed. 'I think the crowd's thirst for blood is now satiated, and they are looking forward to the kill. They expect a quick and clean death. A matador is expected to entertain the crowd with difficult passes and show his prowess. He goes through his apprenticeship as a picador and a banderillero. Only he can put the bull out of its agony by a single stroke of his sabre. If the bull is not killed by the first thrust to his aorta region, then the matador must cut the bull's spinal cord to spare the animal any further pain. If impressed by the final performance, the people applaud as the dead animal is dragged out of the arena.'

A trumpet heralded the final stage of the fight—the matador's one-on-one encounter with the bull when he faces the possibility of being gored to death. The matador met the charge by kneeling on one knee. Other more skilful, dangerous moves followed. At times, he turned his back and walked away, leaving himself particularly vulnerable. The closer he was to the bull's horns, the louder were the cheers. I held my breath in anticipation, watching the drama of colour, grace and courage unfold, thrilled by the matador's passes, my blood tingling at the audience shouting 'Olé!' I admired the agility and skill of the matador. His fluidity of movement and his rhythm.

After exciting the crowd to fever pitch, the matador plunged his sword in between the bull's withers. The bull collapsed.

The matador triumphed in his glory and went around the ring, taking his bows. The fanfare surpassed anything I had previously heard.

Suddenly, the cheering stopped. Silence took over. The bull had risen to its feet. With bloodshot eyes and torn and bleeding body, he bowed to the audience. His legs seemed to crumple beneath him, but he moved on, stopping to bow where the matador had paused to receive his accolades only moments before.

The matador turned to stone—eyes fixed upon the bull he had slain.

Cheers broke out. Even in death, the bull had crowned himself with the matador's laurels!

The bull had died a hero's death.

The picture of the dying bull bowing to the cheers of the audience is forever engraved in my mind. That night, I saw the bull in my dreams. Only then, did I realise how ruthless it had all been. I had been admiring the skill of the matador and had not thought of the barbarity of it all. I recalled watching rodeos in Australia. I used to admire the rider's skill, strength and courage, thinking the bull was bucking because he was trying to get him off its back. I had not been aware cruel methods were often used to make the bull buck even more and excite the crowd.

'When I worked on farms as a boy, someone told me that the flank straps were tied round the bull's testicles,' Colin told me later. 'Whenever the rider tightens his hold on the rope to prevent himself from falling, it squeezes the genitals. At times, a bull is prodded with electric rods just before entering the ring, even while still in the chute. Rodeos can be a cruel sport.'

I was appalled. Fortunately, there are now laws regulating such practices in most states. Queensland is the only state that currently does not have regulations regarding rodeos. It only declares the treatment of animals in rodeos must comply with the Queensland Animal Care and Protection Act of 2001. I hope the practice of placing burrs beneath the flank straps and using electric prods will be strictly enforced all over the world. Sports like bull fighting and rodeos also endanger the lives and limbs of combatants.

The next day we toured the Pyramid of the Sun at Teotihuacan—the world's third largest pyramid and a UNESCO World Heritage site. After climbing the Sun and the Moon pyramids for views of the entire site, we were whisked off to the Shrine of Our Lady of Guadalupe, a Spanish Baroque work of art dating back to the 16th century. We watched penitents crossing the gravelled square of the famous church on their bare knees, amazed at their spirit of penance.

The coach went on to Acapulco, where divers plunging from great heights into the ocean below kept us spellbound. Later, we visited the silver city of Taxco and bought trinkets and bracelets.

Our return trip stopover was Honolulu. The weather was balmy and the people charming. Holiday memories remain entrapped as photographs in our album and in my mind.

The following year, in August 1976, Mum had an operation for cataracts. Sick with worry, I attempted to stifle the spider of anxiety rising within me. But we planned to visit Perth in December, so I refrained from mentioning my fears, and counted the days for the reunion with my family after twenty years.

Mercifully, Mum recovered from the surgery, but it left her weak and tired.

Two months passed. Rose and Pat planned a holiday at Carnarvon to look at the wildflowers. Mum wrote, telling us she would be joining them. They were to pick her up on October 18.

It was not to be. The postman delivered a telegram from Rose, informing us of Mum's death. I slapped my hands against my cheeks and wailed, 'Why didn't Mum wait for me?' Waves of sorrow swelled and crashed, snatching me away from my haven of happiness. Grief seized me and tossed me down on a rocky shore.

The next day, we received a letter written by Mum just two days before she died. 'It was like Mum was still speaking to me as she did in her weekly letters,' I sobbed in Colin's comforting arms.

Numb with grief, we flew to Perth for the funeral. Rose, distraught, met us at the airport. She burst out, 'When we came to pick Mum up for the trip to Carnarvon, black clouds hid the sun. It was dark and windy. Then it started to rain. Such strange weather for October. It turned cold. I shivered and buttoned up my coat. Two birds lay dead on the driveway.' Then, unlike her usual chatty self, she fell silent.

Bertie ran out as soon as he heard the car. He lost no time in telling the story. 'On the morning of Mum's death, I went into her room to check on her.' His voice choked. 'Mum lay on her side with a faint smile on her face, her eyes fixed on a picture of Christ. I took her hand in mine. It was cold.' His eyes filled with unshed tears.

A lump rose to my throat. My heart crumpled. *I was not with Mum when she died!* I had so looked forward to seeing my mother together with the whole family.

I was inconsolable. For weeks after our return home, I read, re-read and wept over all Mum's letters that I had treasured over the years.

'When things did not turn out as she hoped, Mum would often say, *what man proposes, God disposes.*' I sobbed on Colin's shoulder. '*God knows best* was another of her favourites. Now, her words teach me to accept her death.'

Colin held me tight. 'She's gone to a happier place and is at peace.'

My mother's death ended her life, but she had gone ahead of me on the road I will travel to the grave. I will carry the songs she sang to me in the cradle. I will carry her words of advice. Her words of wisdom.

Chapter 7

Queensland, 1976–1986

WE RETURNED TO PERTH IN Christmas 1976. My sister was trying to cope with her two infants aged three and two, while recovering from the trauma of losing our mother. Winston's daughter, Tania, was a year old, and Bertie's wife, Ann, was pregnant. There seemed to be babies and toddlers everywhere, and the memory of our baby flooded back. Our Mary would have been a year older than Rose's elder daughter, Maureen. It was a sad Christmas that year, as we all missed Mum, and I missed both Mum and Mary.

However, the trip helped bond our family. The following year, both my brothers as well as my sister, wrote to me regularly.

In 1978, Bertie phoned to say he would be driving to Canberra with his wife and little son. I looked forward to their visit. Bertie had bought a new red campervan and had driven all the way. He looked tired. His wife, Ann, still retained her good looks. His son, Clive, had a mop of dark curly hair, and I failed to see any resemblance to Bertie, whose hair had been light brown in his youth. But young Clive had inherited his parents' musical talents. He clapped in time to their singing and had already learned to sing in tune with them.

I gave Bertie acupuncture to help him recover from the long journey. Ann was afraid of needles, but Clive said he also wanted needles like his daddy, so I gave him a couple; one on each hand.

He lay on the carpet with his arms outstretched and said, 'Just like Jesus.'

Both Bertie and Ann belonged to the charismatic movement, known for speaking in tongues. My heart went out to Bertie's boy, my only nephew.

Ann was a good cook and had given lessons to Bertie, so he showed me how to prepare some Burmese dishes. We had fun together, and they enjoyed my rosehip jam, made from the 'berries' I had gathered while bushwalking.

All too soon Bertie and I were bidding each other a tearful farewell.

Colin craved more knowledge of his English heritage. In 1980, we travelled to England to meet his relatives who, to that point, were just photos in an album. Colin's mother gave us the addresses of her two brothers Clarence and Roy.

She said, 'You won't remember your cousin Geoff, but you used to romp around together until we left for Australia. He's only a few months older than you. He is a schoolteacher now. His dad was my eldest brother. Roy is the youngest. Clarence's children, June and Paul were born after we left for Australia.'

London was cold and dreary as we visited the famous landmarks. I was particularly impressed by Piccadilly Circus because, as a child, I longed to see the clowns and lions.

One day, we came across a building in ruins with only one of the walls standing among weed-covered debris. 'What happened here?'

'Left over from the Blitz,' Colin replied, a catch in his voice.

I was astonished to think that even after thirty-five years a reminder of those terrible times remained.

After a few days in London, we took the train to Nottingham, Colin's birthplace. His relatives still lived in the suburb where their forefathers had been born and died. Colin flushed with pleasure when he met his relatives.

'You look like our dad when he was young,' Paul said.

'He has the same characteristics—tidiness and meticulousness,' June remarked, when she saw Colin washing the rental car.

Love and affection for family reflected in their faces, and a warm and cosy feeling enveloped me to see Colin with his cousins.

We stayed for a night at Roy's home. He took us sight-seeing and his relaxed and jovial nature drew us to him. Little did we know it would be the last time we would meet on this earth. He died of kidney failure not long after we returned to Australia. We felt we had lost an old friend as well as a relative, although we had only seen him for a few days.

From a distance, Nottingham Castle's exterior conjured up images of former times. Drawing closer, we realised that it was mainly ruins. Only the castle lodge remained standing. We dined at the world-renowned *Ye Olde Trip to Jerusalem* Inn in the Castle. According to legend, Robin Hood and his men frequently made merry there. Hewn out of the rock, the building was composed of caves and dungeons.

Returning to London, saturated with history, we joined Global Tours for a three-week European tour. The windmills in Amsterdam fascinated us; Germany's Heidelberg Castle and Black Forest revived memories of childhood fairy tales.

Snow at Lucerne made a traditional Christmas scene. We watched the church congregation arrive in sleighs and horse-drawn carriages. After Mass we took a train ride up to Mt Rigi. An ermine cloak, furred by snow, covered the pine trees and houses.

On Boxing Day, we toured Salzburg. The town, with its gabled roofs and spires, was a fairy-tale come to life. Salzburg's biggest annual attraction is the Mozart Festival. Music lovers and virtuosos from all over the world come to pay homage to the great musician—the child prodigy, who composed music from the age of five. We visited the Mozart Museum and bought tiny replicas of his piano, violin, and a doll representing the genius himself. His music is happy, serene, flawless and everlasting. Later, when we started going to operas, we never failed to see all his operas whenever they were performed in Brisbane.

We stopped in Europe's musical capital, Vienna, for a few days. The streets and parks are crowded with statues and monuments of world-famous musicians. Houses proudly display plaques showing where Beethoven, Mozart, Brahms, Schubert, and Haydn lived.

Taken to the Schönbrunn Palace on the outskirts of the city, we walked through the palatial rooms. They glittered with gold, silver and crystals and were decorated by tapestries, murals, and oil paintings.

In awe, we absorbed the beauty of the magnificent buildings and statues in Venice and Florence. Two Swiss Guards dressed in yellow and blue vertical striped uniform with plumed helmets, armed with swords and battle-axes, stood guard at the entrance to the Vatican Palace.

The highlight of our Vatican visit was Pope Pius XII standing on the balcony and giving his blessing to the crowds in St Peter's Square. The hushed silence was only broken by the sound of breathing when he was about to bestow his blessing. Microphones magnified the dignified voice that had saved the Vatican from pillage by the Nazis during World War II. Controversially, critics say he sided with the Nazis, but it has been proved he saved many lives by giving refuge to Jews and prisoners-of-war.

We visited St Peter's Basilica, the largest church in the world. We longed to see the catacombs where the early Christians had taken refuge from Roman persecution. However, the tourist bus whisked us off to the casino in Monte Carlo and continued on to Paris. There, we left the tour and boarded a train to Lourdes, as one of my dearest dreams had been to visit the grotto where Our Lady had appeared.

We only stopped for a day at Lourdes, but the sight of so many crutches on one side of the grotto, discarded when crippled people were cured, struck me with force. I was reminded of Our Lord saying, 'Take up thy bed and walk' to the disabled man. A great flood of joy filled me when I saw the spring that had appeared during Our Lady's apparition. The spring that had cured so many dreadful diseases. The spring that brings healing to the soul.

I thought of my mother who was devoted to Mary and wished she could be here with us. But she was in heaven now and enjoyed perfect bliss. My faith in God escalated. I prayed for Colin and all my loved ones. While praying, I tasted the sweetness of the Divine Presence and had a foretaste of Heaven, just as I used to, when praying before the Blessed Sacrament as a novice.

The three-week lightning tour gave us a taste of Europe, and I breathed a contented sigh. 'I've fulfilled my dreams of travelling overseas.'

Colin smiled, little realising it was only the beginning of our travels.

During vacations, Colin and I would pack our campervan and head north to Maryborough, a country town in Queensland, where his dad and mum had retired. We would stay the night with his parents and, after breakfast, leave for Hervey Bay, only half an hour's drive away. We would walk along the foreshore then swim in the calm waters. I loved the peaceful lifestyle. Colin had spent his childhood in Portland, a small country town in Victoria, but I had never experienced country life.

I was pleased with our good jobs and established Naturopathic clinic but Colin was dissatisfied in the Public Service. He spent his working day inspecting new buildings and verifying whether they were constructed according to regulation. He wanted something to satisfy his creative mind.

As a young boy his dream had been to own a farm, grow fruit and nut trees, and keep ducks and chickens. That longing rose again. *Perhaps I could get a teaching position in Maryborough. That would provide a base for us to establish an herb farm and open a naturopathic clinic.*

On one trip, charmed by its rustic atmosphere, we bought a couple of acres in Maryborough, and built a double garage on it. But the land had no dam and, without water, we could not grow herbs, so we hired a team to put in a bore.

Breathless, we watched the drill piercing the soil, delving deeper and deeper until water gushed forth. We cheered and clapped. Colin's Dad shook his hand and his Mum kissed me. One of the workmen cupped some of the water in his hand and sipped it. Spitting it out, he strode towards us. 'Sorry, mate. The water is saline.'

Colin gasped. 'Saline? Useless?'

He nodded. Colin paid him and, with sinking hearts, we watched the men fill the hole. Each shovelful of dirt buried our dreams. When every vestige of our hopes lay deep beneath the soil, we drove to an estate agent and put our property on the market.

We returned home disappointed and dissatisfied. From then on, we would still go up to Maryborough during my school holidays, but we would camp on our property and sleep in our garage. On hindsight, we realise we should have done some research before buying the property, but I was a city girl and knew nothing about such things, and Colin had been too eager to move further north and enjoy life in the country.

After teaching for thirteen years in Canberra, I secured a position in Brisbane in 1984, and we moved there, hoping Colin would soon obtain a job with the State government. To save money, we sent most of our belongings by truck, then drove north with our trailer fully loaded. We planned to go to Sydney via Berrima and take the Pacific Highway to Brisbane.

That day happened to be one of the coldest days on record. A blanket of snow covered the roads and surrounding countryside. I was enjoying the wintry scene when the car wheels lost traction. Colin soon realised the cause. 'We have a flat tyre.'

'How can you change the tyre with all this snow?' I asked.

A service station was not far off. 'Why don't we shelter there?' He parked beneath the awning of the petrol bowsers. Being Sunday, the garage was shut.

I shivered with cold and fear. Fear because we were stranded in the middle of nowhere in a snowstorm. Fear of spending the night in the freezing cold.

Normally, Colin remains calm in emergencies. But now, surrounded by snow, with everything bleak and forbidding, he turned pale. I had never seen him look so helpless. I knew I would have to do something, so I reached out and applied pressure on his 'Revival Point'—an acupressure point.

Within minutes, his colour returned, and we were able to change the tyre.

'We don't have a spare tyre now. If we have another puncture, we will not be able to go on. But we can't stay here in case the snow becomes deeper.'

Colin drove slowly, taking care to keep in the middle of the road. Fortunately, we met no traffic until a few miles out of Berrima, a line of vehicles stopped further progress.

'What's wrong now?' His voice rose in exasperation. 'An accident?'

'Perhaps we should get out and walk around,' I said, seeing other drivers standing beside their cars, stamping their feet to get warm.

We got out and swung our arms to put some heat into our frozen hands. On the other side of the road, a group of truckies stood in a circle outside a café. The aroma of coffee drifted towards us. 'How about coffee?' Colin asked.

I nodded, threw a blanket around myself like a poncho and crossed the road with Colin. We joined the truckies outside the cafe.

'What's holding us up?' Colin asked.

'The hill beyond Berrima is covered by snow and ice. We may slide down the hill and cause an accident,' a truckie informed us.

'Is any other road open?'

'If you make a detour and head for Bowral, you'll get through.'

'Thanks, mate.'

After a cup of coffee, we returned to the car, and took the detour via Bowral. Vestiges of snow still lay around, but the roads were not blocked.

We arrived in Parramatta around 9 pm and found a garage open. A mechanic repaired our tyre and we drove on to Coffs Harbour before checking in at a hotel. The trip from Canberra had taken longer than anticipated but, thanks to God, we had made it.

We bought a house in Hecklemann Street, Carina, close to San Sisto College, where I was to commence teaching at the beginning of the new school term. Our Canberra house had not sold, and the estate agent kept saying it was on the wrong side of the street. 'If it were on the other side, in Chapman, it would have been sold straight away. That is a prestigious suburb.'

So, we were paying off the loan on two houses—at Canberra and Brisbane.

Colin's mother Eva was disappointed we had not settled in Maryborough. She showed her disapproval by never inquiring about my new job, or how we were getting on in Brisbane. In the months that followed, we visited Colin's parents regularly, but our visits grew fewer because his mother's emotions flowed hot and cold without any apparent reason. Sometimes, she would give me a gift like a handbag, and we would buy her a plant for her garden. At other times, she would reproach us for living so far from them. 'You weren't here, so your dad had to rely on your cousin to help him do some repairs on the house.'

'It's not as if we didn't try to move to Maryborough to be near you and dad,' Colin said.

Colin's cousin, Phillip, was living with his parents, Doug and Barbara Dover, who had also chosen to retire in Maryborough. Doug was Eva's youngest brother, who had seen action in North Africa and Italy during World War II. They, too, had migrated from the UK to Portland, Victoria, then to the ACT, and finally to Maryborough. They were the only two members of the Dover family who lived in Australia.

The move from Canberra to Carina had proved stressful, and ill-feeling between Eva and us did not help matters. I guess it was only natural for her to want her son to live close to her, as her daughter, Sharon, had married, and was still living in Canberra.

Colin developed a malignant melanoma on his back, so an operation was performed in August 1984. It left him with a great gash and he could barely move his arms for some time both because of the pain and for fear of the stitches tearing.

When the wound healed, Colin applied for a job in the Queensland Public Service but there were no vacancies. I too, found it difficult to settle at first, even though my pupils were delightful. But my Graduate Diploma in Teaching from the University of New England was not recognised in Queensland.

'I'm a fully qualified teacher, have taught for three years in Perth and 13 years in Canberra, yet I have to be supervised like a trainee teacher. Besides this, a report is written by my supervisor after each lesson. It is even more humiliating than anything I went through as a novice in Burma.' I had spent several years in a novitiate, training to be a nun, where I had been subjected to harsh words and hard work, in an attempt to teach me to be humble and submissive. Obviously, they had failed.

I was so unhappy during my first year at San Sisto I considered resigning. My heart had sung when past students referred to me as their teacher, but no more.

'We can manage financially once we open our Naturopathic Clinic. Then you can give up teaching,' Colin said.

The desire to heal myself and others had driven me to enrol in the Australian College of Acupuncture for a Graduate Diploma. I was given exemption in many units because of my studies in Naturopathy and Biochemistry, and completed the course within two years.

During this time, our home was a mess. Most of our goods were still unpacked because we intended buying a new house once our property in Canberra sold. To make matters worse, after a rainy spell, a spring appeared beneath our old Queenslander and some of the boxes we had stored downstairs were soaked.

I held up a soggy letter to Colin. 'This is one of the last letters Bertie wrote when he lived in the UK. I recognise his writing. Only the date and a few lines are legible!'

In early 1986, Bertie wrote, saying he had been granted Long Service Leave and would be driving out with his wife and son. I was delighted, but I wished we had already moved into a bigger home. Colin hastily made some extensions on the old Queenslander, to provide an extra room for Bertie and his family. Providentially, he had recently managed to secure a job with the Logan City Council as a Building Surveyor.

We took Bertie and his family to an amusement park on the Gold Coast, thinking Clive would enjoy himself, but he was too terrified to ride on the 'Ghost Train.' Ann, too, grew nervous when we drove to Mt Tamborine. She screamed when negotiating the steep walking tracks. Poor Colin was frustrated in his attempts to entertain my family. Only Bertie and I enjoyed ourselves.

But time flew. How I wished that Bertie's Long Service Leave and my school holidays had coincided so that we could have spent more time together. But, as the famous author, Paulo Coelho, said, 'Tears are words that need to be written.'

About a month later, Rose and her husband Pat drove over from Perth in their campervan with their two charming daughters, Maureen and Eileen. Rose had put on a bit of weight since the children's births, but Pat had not changed. He was a typical Irishman with a sense of humour and a love for his Guinness. They first stopped at a caravan park, but then shifted to our garden and used our facilities. They did not stay in the room prepared for them, as they felt they could not impose their little girls on us as well. Seeing my nieces, I once again thought of our Mary, who would have loved to meet her cousins.

I was delighted to see Rose again after ten years. I took leave to be with her, as she would not be staying long.

Our circumstances had changed rapidly. In Canberra, Colin and I both had good jobs as well as a prosperous naturopathic clinic. In Canberra, we had lived in a beautiful Cape Cod design home with air-conditioning and an outdoor glassed-in spa, enabling us to enjoy our garden. Now we lived in an old Queenslander.

Had we done the right thing by moving north?

Chapter 8

The Tyranny of Distance

ALL MY MISGIVINGS ABOUT THE move to Queensland vanished by 1987, when we settled into a colonial-style house with a wraparound verandah to keep us cool in the hot summer months. Our home was on three quarters of an acre, and close to the sea. An Arcadia—a dream realised. We planted exotic tropical fruit trees—mangoes, custard apples, lychee and longan—and bred geese, ducks and hens.

'I used to dream of owning an orchard and farm animals.' Colin's eyes shone like two blue lakes sparkling in the sun.

'Now you have what you always wanted.' I hugged him.

Weekends were adventures. We visited all the theme parks on the Gold Coast and at Sea World, gasping in wonder at the dolphin shows. Our ultimate experience was walking with a fully-grown tiger and its keeper at Dreamworld. Patting the tiger gave me thrills of pleasure. Movie World's 3D experience, the Disney Shows and rides turned us into adrenaline junkies. We hiked in the National Parks on the Gold Coast hinterland, then drove down to the beach for a swim. Hervey Bay and Rainbow Beach became our favourite places for weekends, just as Eden and the Snowy Mountains had been when we lived in Canberra. Happiness enveloped us. We had each other. We had everything we wanted and loved everything we had.

The spring holidays saw us at Alice Springs and Ayers Rock in the Red Centre. At that time, climbing the rock was still permitted, and we found this an exhilarating experience.

'So glad we did this before we grow too old and feeble.' The wind blew with such force on top of the rock I began to feel quite uncomfortable. Fortunately, I carried a few needles in my backpack, so I gave myself acupuncture on the 'wind point,' between the thumb and forefinger, to disperse the wind which had penetrated my body. I felt better immediately.

We stayed at a Youth Hostel with an outdoor toilet. That night, on my way to the toilet, the ghostly light of the moon cast a silvery tinge on the surrounding bushes. Silent as a spectre, a dingo appeared. I will never forget that scene—the dingo with its distinctive walk as if treading on eggs, loping along against the spectral landscape. A shiver passed through my body. It reminded me of another time, so many years ago, in Darjeeling, on a similar moonlit night, when my brother Rupert had awakened me to see a flying fox on a tree. It looked eerie against the background of the snow-covered Himalayas. I had visualised wolves and vampires and was fascinated by the spooky scene.

Rose's elder girl Maureen won a trip to Japan—a prize from the Yamaha Piano Competition, so Rose sent her younger daughter Eileen to us for a holiday during the school break. Eileen had just entered her teens and wore the sweet innocent looks of a child. The modern toxic culture had not yet laid its hand upon her. She loved books, music and cooking, but apart from stacking her beloved books neatly on her bookshelves, her room was always in a sorry mess, so she kept the door of her room shut at home. She did the same with us.

We took her to all the Theme Parks. She was a quiet girl and scarcely spoke, so we hardly got to know her well, but she appeared to have a great time. In 1988, when the World Expo opened in Brisbane, revealing the pleasures of live theatre, we bought ourselves a season's ticket for Expo 88 and invited Eileen over. The three of us had a great time visiting the various pavilions. Excerpts from *My Fair Lady* and *Oliver,* performed at the British Pavilion, ambushed us and entrapped our memories.

When Eileen returned to Perth, we took Colin's parents to see the Tall Ships sail up the Brisbane River, then drove them back to Maryborough.

After Expo had shown us the delights of classical music, we listened to radio stations like 4 MBS and ABC Classical and hankered for live entertainment. Later, we developed a taste for live opera.

Not long after the excitement of Expo had died down, Colin's mother phoned, asking him to collect a purebred pup from a breeder in Brisbane. 'He's not far from where you live. We'll meet you at Yatala and pick her up. I've already made all the necessary arrangements with the man. It will be a Christmas gift for your dad.'

'If you're coming to Brisbane, why don't you stop at our place?' Colin asked.

'No. We'll be going to the Dog Trials in Yatala and will be busy at the Show. Only staying for the day.'

The pup was a typical Golden Labrador—blonde and cuddly. When Colin read her papers, he gasped. 'Her pedigree is as long as your arm. She comes from better stock than either of us.'

We drove over to Yatala with the pup, where Albert and Eva had agreed to meet us, as they wanted to sample the famous Yatala pies.

When Colin handed the pup over to his mother, she said, 'We'll name her Lisa.'

Albert's eyes glistened and his hands trembled when Eva presented Lisa to him.

Opera, Orchids and Oz

On their return to Maryborough, Albert took Lisa for dog-obedience classes. She proved to be an apt pupil and followed him everywhere—to his workshop, garden, and the dinner table. She even slept in his room as Eva had moved to another area because of his snoring. In time, Albert became a trainer himself, and later, he judged events at Dog Shows.

During one of our visits to Maryborough, Eva said, 'Your father gives too much attention to Lisa and neglects me.'

Colin understood his father's need to keep himself occupied and relax after years of hard work but did not want to take sides. 'Dad now has a hobby. It'll keep him from being bored.'

Albert's complexion grew a shade darker. He glared at his wife, then turned to Colin. 'Your mother lies in bed most of the time and refuses to do the housework. She says cleaning-aids bring on an asthma attack.'

Before his mother could say anything further, Colin rose and kissed her. 'Hope your health improves, Mum.'

He gave Lisa a pat and nodded at his Dad. I followed Colin's cue and kissed them goodbye. I was embarrassed. It was the first time I had witnessed an argument between Colin's parents.

A few weeks' later, Albert phoned. 'Your Mum's sight is failing, and she has to come to Brisbane to see a specialist.'

They drove down and stayed with us until the tests were done. 'I'm going blind,' Eva said. 'My doctor has recommended special visual aids. I'll need them soon.'

Her words wrenched our hearts. Life without sight would indeed be a burden on both of them.

Albert had owned the puppy for three months when, during one of our visits, Eva took Colin aside. 'I'm sending Lisa for training as a guide dog. She'll be useful to me when I'm blind.'

Colin knew that Lisa meant more to his Dad than anything else in the world, so he tried to dissuade her. She remained silent but fortunately, the matter died down as soon as it raised its ugly head. Lisa remained Albert's faithful companion until death parted them.

Eva had many mood swings. She had long passed menopause so we both knew the swift changes in her temperament were not due to that. A few months before her death, the specialist discovered their cause—pernicious anaemia. A course of B12 injections stabilised her moods. Too late, she became a dear, sweet mother but her moods had already created dissension within the family. Had doctors known of her problem earlier, there may have been less tension between everyone.

Eva's eyesight did not deteriorate, but her last year was painful. Continually in and out of hospital, she cheerfully lined her prescription tablets on the dinner table showing us they measured over a foot in length. She had confidence in her doctors and took her medication faithfully. We hated drugs of any sort, whether recreational or prescribed, but we knew it was useless to explain that many medications do more harm than good.

Colin's Uncle Doug also fell seriously ill. He had retired from the meatworks in Portland and received a compensation payout due to work-related emphysema. He had bought a house in Maryborough and settled down with his wife Barbara. We liked his jovial nature, and still recall one of his last wisecracks when he'd been speaking about spring. Frail, and with his breath coming in short gasps, Doug said, 'I know that spring-feeling. I sometimes get it too but wonder what it is.'

Doug brought out the best in his sister. They used to joke about who would ultimately beat the other in the race to the next world.

One night we received an urgent phone call from Colin's Dad. 'Mum is not expected to survive until tomorrow morning.'

'I'll be with you as soon as I can get there.' Colin passed the news to me, dressed, got in the car, and raced to Maryborough.

Within two days, his mother rallied, so Colin returned home.

The next time Eva was admitted into hospital, we drove up to Maryborough. She complained of a pain in her upper back and sighed with relief as we took turns massaging the area. Our hearts ached to see her suffer and we both realised the end was near.

She died in June 1989, a few days after our visit.

Albert hardly ever showed his emotions, but his feelings surfaced at the cemetery. Tears coursed down his rugged features and his face crumpled. It lasted for a few moments then disappeared—interred forever in his wife's grave.

Colin's father had submitted to his wife throughout their marriage. He must have loved her because he had proved it by his patience, hard-work and catering to her whims.

Too ill to attend the funeral, Colin's uncle, Doug, realised he would soon be joining his sister. He died a few months later.

I felt guilty about my harsh feelings towards Eva but, from then on, when people behaved badly, I always wondered whether their behaviour was triggered by illness.

On 9 November, the radio blared out news of the fall of the Berlin Wall. Colin and I rushed to the lounge and turned on the television. Pictures of crowds climbing over the wall were being shown on every channel. It seemed like God had answered the prayers of the faithful and Russia had been converted. We gazed wide-eyed at each other. *Miracles still happen!* We joined in the joy of the crowds, and hugged each other.

The Falling of the Wall led to the Malta Summit Conference between US President George Bush and Soviet General Secretary Mikhail Gorbachev in December. Within two days, they declared an end to the Cold War. I recalled the sense of freedom I had experienced when Britain had freed Burma from Japan in 1945. I also remembered my delight when we had fled from father in

August 1952, and again in 1967, when I had escaped from the Burmese military government and taken refuge in Australia.

This world event of 1989, as well as the international exhibitions at Expo in 1988, brought on itchy feet. We flew to Singapore the following year, and visited Fort Silo, that impregnable fortress the British had relied upon to withstand Japanese invasion in 1941. One of the coastal batteries in southern Singapore, it had since been restored as a military museum, housing photos of the Japanese invasion. It was only after its fall, when all hope of saving Burma had been lost that my parents made hasty plans for evacuation. My father held on until the British ordered all government officials to evacuate either to India or to Katha further north. We chose Katha, but when the Japanese bombed the town, we had to flee again.

During our first visit to Singapore, we also visited the botanical garden, marvelling at the beautiful orchids. At the time we had not dreamt of growing them, but I had always loved flowers. Even as a toddler, I would never sit still for long, unless I was seated among the blooms. All my infant photos were of me amid flowers. Unfortunately, we do not have any photographic mementoes because, although Mum had saved our albums when we evacuated from Rangoon, they were left behind in Katha.

In 1991, we visited Singapore again. This time, we took the bus to Kuala Lumpur and Malacca. Being a builder, Colin was interested in the town hall at Malacca, built in the Dutch colonial style. I was fascinated by the place where Saint Francis Xavier, patron saint of missionaries, was buried because, during my convent days, I had longed to be a missionary and convert souls to Christ.

The next year we flew to Fiji. Shocked at the sight of huge cauldrons the Fijians used to boil their enemies during their cannibal days, I shuddered. A huge Fijian grabbed a spear and leapt at me so suddenly I stepped back in fear, before realising it was an act for the tourists.

Friendly Fijians invited us home to taste their famous native brew—kava. They were so hospitable and cheerful—a great contrast to eating their enemies in the old days. I grew jolly and talkative, like the time I had been drunk when some novices had given me a glass of home-brewed rice-wine at a mission-station on the hills.

Colin felt a sense of guilt for taking me away from my good teaching job in Perth to Canberra in 1970. Then again, after I had settled down happily in Canberra, we had moved to Queensland. The parting from my family in Perth had wrenched my heart. Moving to Queensland had been difficult too—I had left an excellent job and good friends. Colin was so relieved when, after the initial setbacks, my teaching qualifications were at last recognised in Queensland, and I grew to love my job.

In 1991, because I taught Religious Education at San Sisto College, the Catholic Education Office granted me six months' Sabbatical leave on full pay to study for my Associate Diploma Course in Theology. Appreciating the break from teaching, I attended lectures and studied in a serene campus. 'My immersion in religious studies brought back to mind my days in the novitiate,' I said to Colin. 'I have the best of both worlds—the peace and tranquillity of a spiritual life as well as the joys of marriage.'

In the novitiate, we had focussed more on the three vows of Poverty, Chastity and Obedience that we would take after three years of training. During the Theology course, we studied the deeper philosophical ideas of theologians like John Henry Newman and more ancient ones like Thomas Aquinas, so I grew to understand my religion even more. I was grateful to the Department of Catholic Education for the time off, but grew dissatisfied when, because student numbers were falling, I was transferred to a co-educational school.

The tyranny of distance prevented my family from meeting together as often as I wanted.

In September 1990, Rose and Pat invited us to Perth. I begged Colin to accept. 'It will be so much like old times when we went around carol-singing in Mandalay.'

l was overjoyed to meet Rose after so long. During the past few years, my sister had been busy caring for her two daughters, and I had been enjoying life with Colin, so we had drifted apart. The visit strengthened our ties.

Pat drove us to King's Park. The wildflowers were in bloom. I recalled the farewell dinner of twenty years ago, with Mum, Rose, Pat and Winston when I had left Perth for Canberra with Colin, and my heart was torn in two because Mum was no longer with us.

Rose generously lent us their car while they were at work. We visited Rottnest Island and were thrilled with the quokkas. We cycled around on a tandem bike. It reminded me of the song, *Daisy, Daisy,* Mum used to sing about two lovers who rode a bicycle built for two.

As Bertie was at work, I did not get to see him. He did not visit Rose's house as there had been a rift between them, and he felt unwelcome. I decided it would be wrong to use Rose's car to visit him in the evenings as they were estranged. So I was overjoyed when he came to see me off at the airport.

Neither did I get to see Winston. He worked as a psychiatrist nurse on shift at a mental hospital. His wife had left him and taken their two daughters, so he suffered bouts of depression. He spent his life between work and the gym and chose to isolate himself from friends and family.

In July 1992, the next year, Rose and Pat flew up to Cairns. Glad at the chance to meet my sister again, if only for a short while, we drove to Brisbane airport to have a few hours with them during their stopover.

Travel lust struck again and we toured China in 1994. We flew to Beijing, and the tourist bus took us to the Great Wall. Built to keep out invaders from the north, the wall winds its way across China through deserts, grasslands, mountains and plateaus.

It took us about 45 minutes to ascend the hill to the winding stone walkways along the Zheng Guan Terrace with its three watch towers. The Great Wall at Mytianya is the best-preserved section and spans over a mile. As we trekked along, we witnessed a combination of man-made wonder and nature wilderness.

After enjoying fabulous mountain views from the ancient stronghold, we were taken to a restaurant to sample the famous Peking Duck. There we met a couple from Brisbane on the same tour. I was destined to meet Margaret Dakin again when I joined her writing group—the Vineyard Writing Group—and also at the Victoria Point Library Group.

Margaret excels in writing short stories and won the Redlitzer Competition in 2013. It is a privilege to be her friend.

Fully satiated after our sumptuous dinner in Beijing, we were driven to the iconic Tiananmen Square and the Forbidden City—home to China's emperors for 400 years. I bought several souvenirs, including a replica of the Great Wall. I sent one to Rose, and also posted photos of our trip to Bertie and Winston.

On our return, Colin and I continued to see Albert in Maryborough. We would visit Eva's grave and then drive on to Harvey Bay for a swim before returning home.

That year, 'mad cow disease' hit the UK. Colin's cousin wrote, saying the family had turned vegetarian for fear of catching the disease. The following year, news of the first human death from 'mad cow disease' reached us. It came to be known as Creutzfeldt-Jakob Disease in humans. We were concerned about Colin's relatives in the UK and wondered how Albert felt about his two sisters back there—whether he too worried over their danger. But he was a silent man and seldom shared his thoughts. He was kind, though, and soon took the place of the father I had never loved.

Chapter 9

Colin's Dad

EVERY WEEKEND WE VISITED COLIN'S dad in Maryborough. On our arrival, Lisa's tail would wag so much I wondered if it would fall off. A joy to Albert in his old age, she gave him much happiness.

Albert lived in a three-bedroom Queenslander. Doris, an old family friend from Portland who had lost her husband years back, would come to Maryborough every winter and stay with Colin's parents. She continued her visits even after Eva's death.

Early in 1995, some six years after Eva had passed away, Albert said, 'I've been thinking of buying a caravan and going on a camping trip all over Australia with Doris and Lisa. Doris and I love the country.' His eyes lit up and a breath of fresh air seemed to waft into the room.

'Why don't you sell the house and follow your dreams?' Colin asked.

'I can't. Not right now. Lisa has won the first prize in the Labrador section and has been proclaimed Top Dog in Queensland. It's a pity to stop while she's doing so well despite her limp from arthritis. I must enter her in shows as long as she's capable of winning.' Pride in his dog prevented Albert from quitting the Kennel Club and doing his round-Australia trip. He kept postponing it until it was too late.

Albert had been suffering excruciating agony in his right shoulder. The doctor had prescribed medication for arthritis, but tides of pain still ebbed and flowed through his arm, making life a sea of suffering.

His G.P. eventually referred him to an oncologist in Brisbane, so we brought Albert and Lisa to our home, and accompanied him to the specialist. Tests showed cancer of the lungs insidiously spreading throughout every organ in his body. He had hidden his pain from us until the tumour had firmly entrenched itself in every organ.

We tried to make his last days happy. He had not been to the cinema for years, so we took him to *Rob Roy*.

He cheered the actor on. 'Go on, Rob. Go on,' he yelled, as if at a football match.

Albert was a keen gardener, and during his stay with us, he taught me how to prune our citrus trees. He'd say, 'This branch is unhealthy. Just cut it off and let the sun, shine on the rest of the branches.'

I had never loved my own father because of his cruelty, but I grew quite fond of Colin's Dad. I queried him about his ancestors, knowing this was my only chance of obtaining information before he passed away.

'Colin's great-grandmother was a beautiful lady. Everyone loved her. I know little of her, except that one day while picking roses, she pricked her finger on a thorn and carked it.'

At first, Colin was struck dumb with surprise. 'Did she die of blood poisoning?'

Albert nodded. 'I hardly knew my grandparents, but both were colourful characters. Your great-grandfather, Edward Hemingway, was a forceful man who took what he wanted and did what he liked. He would turn up at a relative's place at any hour of the day or night, expecting a hot meal and a comfortable bed. He ruled everyone with an iron hand and feared no one except his wife.'

Colin glanced at me; his eyes open wide. He had obviously not heard this before.

'When the old man was on his deathbed in Nottingham,' Albert continued, 'the family gathered around in silence and gazed down at his pale and motionless body, thinking his spirit had left. As my father bent to feel his pulse, he sat up, flailing his arms and shouted, "I fought with the devil and beat the bastard." He looked triumphant. Then he fell back on his bed and died.'

'What about Grandma?' Colin asked, eager to hear something unusual about her too.

Albert laughed. 'Your grandmother, Martha, had solid middle-class connections. She was fiercely independent and would put people in their proper place. Everyone was afraid of her.' He chuckled. 'She once reprimanded the local police constable for aspiring above his station in life.'

Colin's eyebrows shot up. 'What had he done?'

'One day, she met him doing his beat on the streets and pointed to the gutter. "This is where you walk, young man." The policeman stepped from the pavement without a murmur.'

Neither of us had realised the class system was so widespread even among the middle and working class in England.

Colin tried to pry more information from him. 'Mum said she had knitted shawls and rugs for me.'

'Yes, the old girl kept knitting until she could no longer hold the needles. She suffered from arthritis, you know.'

'I remember collecting our mail from the Post Office. She used to send us the local Nottingham paper.' Colin rubbed his hands together. 'She'd put a little present in the roll of newspaper. A lolly for me, or a trinket for Mum. The papers came as regularly as clockwork.'

During his father's final days, Colin saw his parents in a new light. Their hearts must have always remained at home. Starving for news, they had devoured the Nottingham papers. I guess it was hard—much harder than today to leave Old Blighty.

When Colin reached his half century, he met relatives in the 'Old Country' who lived in the same suburb as their forefathers. He realised for the first time how difficult his parents must have found it to put down roots when they moved to the other side of the world.

As a child in Portland, when playing alone among the tombstones, Colin often sensed the presence of another boy, and even caught a glimpse of him at times. Afraid of ridicule, he never told his Mum of this, but he revealed his secret to me.

'I wonder who kept me company during my childhood days?' Colin mused.

'During our early days of marriage, your Mum often spoke to me of you,' I had replied. 'Once, she told me that she'd had a miscarriage, but it was only a mass of hair.'

Anxious to know the truth when Albert was near the end, I asked, 'Did Colin ever have a brother?'

'Yes. He did. His brother was stillborn two years before Colin's birth.'

Did Colin's brother keep him company during his childhood days?

Albert rarely spoke of his life in the army but during his final days, he recalled the war without any prompting. 'When serving in France, I received a telegram from your mother. It read: *Mum died.* The officer in charge, thinking *my* mother had died, granted me leave, but gave orders to report back on December 24. The telegram referred to my mother-in-law. I attended her funeral, but the temptation to celebrate Christmas with family and friends proved too much and I overstayed my leave. The AWOL cost me fourteen days in the army jail at the Glasgow Gorbals, one of Europe's worst slums. On my way to jail, the locals offered to over-power the guards and release me. "Only give the word, mate, and you're free," they said. I shook my head to indicate I didn't want any further trouble with the law, so my would-be rescuers let the military police pass, unmolested. I spent time polishing dustbin lids but having Christmas with your Mum was worth it.'

Then he fell silent, probably thinking he would soon be joining her for eternity. After a long pause, he continued, 'At the frontline in Germany, I was given guard duties and ordered to round up the prisoners for shipping out. German wireless stations played *Lili Marlene* up to thirty times a day and it became the Second World War's classic song. Both friend and foe sang it. I learned it as well as other songs from the prisoners-of-war, and eventually could sing it in German. I'd join the prisoners in their card games and treat them more as friends than enemies. One of the men gave me his pack of German cards in a leather case as a parting gift. I've kept it all these years. I know you'll treasure it when I've gone.' He paused and swallowed, as though a hard lump had stuck in his throat. 'When peace was declared, our officers ordered us to respect our former enemy. Our duties then changed from armed aggression to controlled occupation. One day, I discovered piles of now-useless German currency at a Post Office. We lit our cigarettes with million-mark notes and boarded a fire engine. With sirens blaring and lights flashing, we raced around. A couple of Military Police signalled us to stop and gave orders to return the engine to the Fire Station straight away. On the way back, I found a typewriter in an abandoned German building and lugged it for miles until I reached a military check point in Ostend. The police ordered me to dump it in a ditch, so I heaved it over. After all my hard work, the typewriter lay among all the other things we'd picked up during our advance into Europe.' He shrugged. A habit he had probably picked up in France. 'The eleventh commandment applied in those days.'

Colin raised his brows. 'What's the eleventh commandment?'

'Thou shall not get caught.'

When I heard these words, I thought of Shakespeare's play, *Henry V*. The king had ordered his men not to harm or pillage the conquered French population and declared that anyone caught stealing would receive the death penalty. The laws were not so harsh during World War II, but the loss of his typewriter seemed unfair to Albert, who considered it one of the spoils of war.

Albert hated war, not only for the horrors he had witnessed, but also because of the way he was treated at the end of hostilities. 'We obeyed orders and shot at the enemy, but all we really wanted was to go home to our families and get on with life.' With a faraway look in his eyes, he continued, 'In July 1946, we received our release papers. After all we had gone through during the war, we were just given a five-bob-suit and a second-class ticket home. If you died, they sent the family a bill for the blanket you were buried in.'

He never got over the demobilisation process. 'One hot day after the war, when building a chimney, I ripped the shoulder titles and colour badges off my shirt and put them in a layer of cement. Then I laid the bricks on top. I wanted to forget the war and have nothing more to do with the army.'

Having lived through the war in Burma, I empathised with him. At the end of hostilities there, I too simply wanted to forget.

Albert's cancer continued to grow. He lost his energy and zest for life. I finished work at 3:00 pm, so I would drive him to the doctor and chemist. When painkillers like Panadol Forte no longer worked, the oncologist prescribed morphine. Albert took his medication cheerfully but spent most of the day asleep in an armchair. We realised he would soon need someone to nurse him. When his faithful friend, Doris, flew up from Portland and offered to look after Albert, we took him back to Maryborough and left him in his own home to enjoy the company and care of a dear friend.

'Give Lisa a home when I've gone,' he said, before parting. 'If you can't keep her, put her down. There's no one else I can trust her with.'

'We'd love to have her.' Colin knew his dad was giving him the dearest possession he had.

Within a few weeks, he was a living skeleton. The bridge of time swept away his hope of happiness and carried him down the dark stream of despair. I asked whether he needed to see any minister of religion, but he declined the offer. Our hearts ached when we saw the state he was in, but it would not do to let him see our sympathy. He perked up when all his friends from the Kennel Club came from as far away as Gympie and Bundaberg to say their goodbyes.

Albert died two days later. Although he had been a loner during most of his life, hundreds turned up for his funeral. Representatives from the Returned Services League performed a touching graveside ceremony and each mourner stepped forward to place a poppy on his coffin.

We gave Lisa a home until her arthritis and pain became too unbearable, but eventually, we had to put her down. I swallowed hard and stroked her as the vet administered the fatal dose. Lisa wagged her tail and left to join her master in the next world.

After his dad's death, in June 1995, Colin wrote to the War Office in London and claimed his medals. He had them mounted and placed in a display cabinet—their bright ribbons were like an attractive rainbow after a storm.

Colin and I grew even closer to each other, following the passing of our parents. Our lives intertwined, and we were inseparable. After my graduation from the Acupuncture College, Colin drew up a plan for a clinic with a waiting room, a consulting room and four treatment rooms. Soon after, I enrolled in the Donsbach University at California as an off-campus student, and obtained a Master of Science in Nutrition, thus adding to my knowledge of natural medicine. I found fulfillment in helping to cure people and relieve their sufferings, but I still longed to write—to put my life down on paper and present it to the world. As the author Anaïs Nin says, 'We write to taste life twice; in the moment and in retrospect.'

Writing helped expose various aspects of myself and helped me experience wholeness and joy. Perhaps it may also help others find comfort and hope amid their sufferings.

Chapter 10

Visits to Perth, 1993–1998

AFTER MUM'S DEATH, WE VISITED Perth several times. In December 1993, Rose and Pat invited us back for a family reunion. After leaving Burma, my Christmases had been spent alone, until Colin and I celebrated together. Christmas with him is always delightful. Delightful and romantic. I never feel lonely. Still, Christmas is a time for family re-unions, and I felt a twinge of sadness at not being all together again.

Rose and Pat said they would meet us at the airport on Christmas morning, but our plane flew in at midnight, and I wondered whether they would be there at such an untimely hour. *What would Colin think of my family if no one met us at the airport as promised?* I recalled the time when I had first arrived in Perth. It was two a.m. in 1967 on a cold, windy morning. Father Foley, from the Catholic Mission Society, had been there to welcome me. I will never forget the relief that had engulfed me.

I need not have worried. Rose and Pat were waiting for us. They greeted us warmly and took us home. As Pat drove past the church, the bells pealed out merrily.

My sister showed us to our room and suggested we go straight to bed as we would be attending Mass at 8 a.m. We passed the Christmas tree laden with gifts. Christmas crackers lay, golden and glistening, on the table. I remained awake for a while, too excited to fall asleep.

After Mass and breakfast, we all gathered around the tree, and presented each other with gifts. Pat, Rose and their two daughters, Maureen and Eileen, as well as the family dog, Indy shared their joy with us. We did not say much, but I recalled one Christmas back in Burma, when my father, in a drunken rage, had used a long sword to cut down the streamers, shouting, 'There will be no more Christmases in *this* house!'

I had been heart-broken at the thought of not celebrating Christmas any longer. But all that was over now.

Everyone came to Rose and Pat's place for a traditional Christmas dinner. Bertie arrived first, with Ann and Clive. Then Winston rolled up. Wanting to have a re-union with the entire family, Rose had also invited his ex-wife Lee and their two daughters, Tania and Sheree. After a while, Lee breezed in with the two girls.

I remember the Christmas tree vainly trying to spread a spirit of gaiety over that hallowed scene. Lee was sitting next to Winston on a sofa, blowing cigarette smoke on his face. He had given up alcohol and cigarettes, hoping she would return, but to no avail. Bertie and his wife sat next to me, Rose and Pat were together, and the five cousins were mingling after a long absence. Our fractured family was together again, if only for a few hours. It seemed that Mum's spirit was with us, as a truce was called, and peace temporarily restored.

We had been close-knit during the war years. I thought of the happy times, and wept inwardly that friction had arisen. The widening gap between each of us caused me pain. Pain that almost smothered my joy at this family gathering. Perhaps our sufferings had bonded us, but we were now divided, not only by distance but by our different goals. Each seemed to go on their separate ways.

Bertie and his wife were besotted by their only child. They bought him a harp to develop his musical talents, sent him to a Catholic school, and endeavoured to give him a good Christian upbringing. Rose adored her two girls and sent them for piano and ballet classes. Winston had brought his girls up with a firm hand, but had taken after his father and drank heavily. All three of my siblings worked hard to support their families, but they had slowly drifted apart.

Rose, always a family-loving person, seemed happy to see us all under her roof. It must have been like the old Burma days, after we had fled from father and lived in harmony until civil war ravaged the country.

Bertie always loved peace and appeared glad to see everyone again. He had been like an Atlas, bearing the weight of the family on his shoulders when our father had thrown him out one Christmas night in Burma.

We spent Boxing Day at the beach with Rose and her family. The following night Bertie and Ann invited the family for dinner and a musical evening. Winston said he was on duty and could not make it, but Rose and Pat came. Ann made some delicious Burmese dishes, as well as roast pork with all the trimmings. After dinner, Bertie strummed his guitar, and we sang all the old Christmas carols. Christmas was a time of festivity. A time for family gatherings. A time for joy.

A lump rose to my throat as we broke into *Silent Night*. It reminded me of the time when Bertie had taken me carol singing with a group of friends.

Rose and Pat took us to a friend's place to bring in the New Year. We danced until the minute hand of the clock neared twelve. Then we formed a circle and joined hands to sing *Auld Lang Syne*. I had been thrilled to dance with Colin and show off the steps we had learned in the early days of our marriage.

We will never forget that jolly Christmastide. That visit remains one of my most treasured memories. It renewed the bond with my family despite the distance. We visited Perth several times after that, but that Christmas season was the last time we four siblings celebrated Christmas together. Winston slowly shrank into himself.

Shrank into his own world from that day.

Chapter 11

Opera, an Opiate, 1995–1998

AFTER OUR PARENTS' DEATHS IN 1995, we lost our faith in traditional medicine. Colin's parents had died despite all the drugs administered by doctors, yet I had survived after a near-death experience by taking herbs and vitamins. My liver was now back to normal, although my cough persisted.

I continued teaching and worked in our after-hours natural therapy clinic from 4 to 6 p.m. Patients often recommended their friends. The clinic grew. However, at my new co-educational school, the boys were unruly. It appeared they were doing their best to show their defiance of authority before the girls, to prove how brave they were.

Some students goaded me. 'Are you Chinese or Japanese?' Their insolent behaviour was so unlike the gentle ways of my students from girls' colleges. My stress levels escalated with each taunt and affront. I found it a challenge to teach in a co-ed school and snapped at them like a caged beast, knowing I was heading for a nervous breakdown if I remained there much longer.

One day, when a male student made an indecent gesture, I went on sick leave, refused to return, and applied for work in a girls' college. I consulted a psychiatrist and told him about the behaviour of some of the male students—their sexual overtones, their insolent behaviour, their disruptive games. Over the course of several consultations, I also mentioned the sexual harassment I had endured from my father in my early teens. The psychiatrist advised me to apply for compensation on the grounds of work-related stress and keep demanding a transfer to a girls' college.

My employers were willing to transfer me to a nearby school, but it was also co-ed. I refused the offer.

After I had used all my sick leave, an official from the Catholic Education Office phoned, telling me to return to work, or my salary would cease. Once again, I reiterated I would not return unless I was given a position at an all-girls' college.

It was during my sick leave that Colin's dad had stayed with us for six weeks, so I was able to take him to the doctor for his morphine scripts. His dog, Lisa, would accompany us whenever we drove down to the chemists too. Their companionship helped pass the time while Colin was at work.

The break from teaching gave me time to recuperate and, towards the end of the year, I was temporarily sent to a girls' school. The following year, I was transferred to St John Fisher at Bracken Ridge. The principal was a model of perfection to her staff, and the pupils a joy to teach.

I saw my psychiatrist once more after that. He recommended going to opera as a therapy. 'Once you have seen an opera, you will discover the healing power of music. Even Shakespeare said that music is the food of the soul.'

I discussed the matter with Colin, and we thought about it. Meanwhile, work in my clinic prospered.

In April 1996, a major tragedy struck Australia. The Port Arthur massacre had its impact on the whole country. The Howard Government introduced uniform gun laws, and Colin had to surrender the cherished rifle of his boyhood days. I suffered with him as I knew how attached he was to it.

The Port Arthur massacre shattered my sense of security. I thought of those who had lost their lives and their bereaved families. It all seemed so senseless. It was fortunate that my sister and her family, who had visited Port Arthur only a few months prior, had not been there when the shootings took place. They could have been among the dead or wounded. *How would I have felt if I lost my sister and her whole family?*

When we saw how unexpectedly one's life could end, we decided to follow my psychiatrist's advice and buy tickets for the opera *Turandot* by Puccini, to be performed at the Lyric Theatre in Brisbane that year. As it was our first experience of opera, we were advised to sit further back because it would be easier to leave if it did not appeal to us.

In trepidation, we entered the theatre, wondering whether it would be a waste of time and money. We had read the story beforehand—the story of a princess who poses three riddles to her suitors. I did not concentrate on the words, but focussed on the music, the singing, and the acting. Puccini's music is uplifting, enchanting, sweeping. When the first strains of the orchestra began the overture, I came close to drowning in the vigour of the singers' voices. Carried up by surges of ecstasy, I was swept away in a wave of passion. It seemed incredible that music could take me out of my body and raise me aloft.

Turandot began our love of opera. I had previously experienced spiritual joy when singing hymns in chapel as a novice. I experience physical ecstasy with Colin, but now my mind floated away in complete abandon. I could hardly believe that music could have such an effect.

Colin, too, enjoyed the opera, so we lost no time in buying tickets for the 1997 opera season. We joined the Opera Club as it would guarantee us the best seats. At pre-opera talks, we became familiar with musical terms as well as the motifs, the players, and the plots.

That was the beginning of a life of sheer luxury. We were invited to opera rehearsals, afternoon teas and cocktail parties. We met the performers and, at intervals, were ushered to a reception room for wine and refreshments and introduced to other members. A friendship soon developed between a particular couple—Tony and his wife Jen. We had many delightful times, and often arranged to meet for dinner at South Bank before a performance.

The season opened with Saint-Saens's *Samson et Dalila*. The opera recounts the biblical struggle between the Hebrews and the Philistines. I was fascinated by the beauty of the singing. The soprano's voice ranged from powerful outbursts to stage whispers, and I marvelled at the preciseness of her diction. The tenor and the rest of the male cast sang with gusto. We had expected to hear something like Puccini's *Turandot,* and came away disappointed because the music had not affected us as much.

Next was *La Bohème* by Puccini, one of the world's most frequently performed operas. Its soaring tunes and passionate romance appealed to novices like us. The score sparkled with wit and was eloquent in love.

Don Pasquale's *Donizetti* was a world-class opera in the bel canto style, requiring agility and flexibility in the singer. The soprano had full even tones and a clear diction, and the tenor projected his melliferous voice well. Much to our delight, the patter in the duet between the bass and the baritone in *Cheti, cheti, imantinante*, was skilfully executed by both singers.

Our last opera that season was Verdi's *Falstaff*. It was an audio-visual feast. Verdi had injected the great Falstaff of Shakespeare's Henry IV into the Falstaff of the *Merry Wives of Windsor,* and the wit and liveliness were extraordinary. Colin and I love all Verdi's operas and Shakespeare's plays. We enjoyed Queensland's 1997 season of opera *buffa*, quickly becoming addicts. As Brisbane held no more than four performances a year, we teamed up with other opera members and booked group-tickets for performances in Sydney. We lived life to the full and returned to Brisbane drunk with happiness.

Our favourite composers were Puccini, Verdi and Mozart. We never missed any of their operas. Colin's favourite opera was Puccini's *Madame Butterfly*. My favourite was *La Traviata*. I loved Verdi's operas best as they were uplifting and stirred the very depths of my soul. Later, when we joined the Wagner Society, I also found Wagner's music stimulating. I never imagined that opera could have such an effect on my emotions. It was an opiate.

Colin's job entailed driving around inspecting houses, then returning to his office to write reports. The long hours of sitting aggravated his back problems. Our belief in natural medicine led him to seek treatment from a chiropractor and an acupuncturist, but he obtained no relief. I recall one night when he cried out, 'If I were a dog I'd be shot.'

My heart bled for him. I gave him Panadol tablets. Next morning, I drove him to the doctor who administered a pethidine injection and referred him to a neurosurgeon. The specialist recommended an operation and made a date for one as soon as he could.

Meanwhile, Colin kept working. Sometimes, he would drop home in between inspections, stagger out of his car, take a dose of Nurofen and collapse into bed. Some mornings, unable to walk, he crawled across the floor to the toilet.

Wrenched by grief, I would phone his office. 'Sorry, Colin won't be in this morning. His back is giving him trouble.'

Will an operation help? What if it's unsuccessful? Will my darling husband be the same? Will he end up in a wheelchair?

He'll be overcome with grief if he ever has to give up bushwalking. God, please help him, I prayed.

Finally, the day of the appointment with the orthopaedic surgeon arrived. His verdict was for an immediate operation, so I drove Colin to hospital, my pulse racing.

After Colin's operation, the surgeon told him the herniated discs at his second and third lumbar vertebrae had caused some fluid to ooze out and solidify, causing the jagged end to act like a saw whenever it touched a nerve.

'Be careful of causing further injury to your back,' the surgeon advised at Colin's final check-up after the operation.

Colin's pain vanished after the procedure, but it left him stiff and sore. He returned to work after months of physiotherapy and decided that the building industry was not for him. He enrolled as a part-time student to study acupuncture. He gained distinctions in biochemistry and anatomy. Impatient to complete his degree, he resigned from work and entered college as a full-time student.

Two years' later, he completed his Bachelor in Acupuncture, and set up a practice. His expertise and sympathetic ear performed miracles. Women would unload their troubles to him. I recall one patient who wished to fall pregnant without having to resort to in-vitro fertilisation. Colin prescribed Chinese herbs and gave her acupuncture and she fell pregnant within a few months.

She visited him after the baby's birth. 'Here's your baby.' She thrust the infant into Colin's arms.

The proud husband held a bouquet of flowers behind his back, waiting patiently until Colin had handed the baby back to the grateful client. 'Thank you,' he said, presenting the bouquet.

Even after years of practice, no patient of mine had ever shown such gratitude. I flushed with pride for Colin. He did well in everything.

When I related the story to my friends, they laughed. 'How *did* he help her fall pregnant?' they asked.

Colin now spent his time working in the clinic. He also started trading on the share market and became adept at analysing Japanese candlesticks or column graphs to predict the direction the market would head.

After teaching for over 25 years, I took early retirement at the end of 1998. Apart from the long drive to school, my final years of teaching were blissful, but I could not resist the offer of a retirement package offered to ten senior teachers.

I devoted my spare time to writing my memoir. It involved researching the history of World War II. Aroused by a desire to visit Kanchanaburi, where prisoners-of-war had lost their lives, we booked a two-week tour of Thailand in the summer of 1999.

Thailand was similar to the country of my birth. I wanted to see the places where Allied soldiers had worked like slaves and where my eldest brother's friend lost his life. We waited at Kanchanaburi Station, amazed at the arid surroundings. 'This is like the soil around Mandalay. The vegetation is so sparse and the terrain dusty and dry.'

The train steamed in and we hurried aboard to secure a good seat for viewing the railway cuttings, where Allied prisoners-of-war had toiled and so many lives were lost. We disembarked at Thanbyuzayat and strolled over the River Kwai Bridge. Two spans had been destroyed by Allied bombs, but they had been rebuilt.

We wandered around the war cemetery before going to the museum. The reconstructed prison camps and photos of skin-and-bone prisoners-of-war gave us insight into the hardships faced by the inmates. Choked by emotion, I thought of the beatings, the beriberi, the beheadings. I scarcely spoke.

On our return to Kanchanaburi, I broke the silence. 'My eldest brother, Rupert, was taken away by the Japanese troops as forced labour when he was young, but he escaped and returned home. His friend, who was also taken by the Japanese, lies buried somewhere near the railroad.'

Colin squeezed my hand.

'It must have been difficult for anyone to find the last resting place of their loved one. If Rupert had not managed to escape, his body could have been among these graves too,' I concluded.

Colin put a protective arm around me, and I drew strength from his loving understanding.

From Changmai we drove on a few miles to the Salween River—the border between Thailand and Burma. We had no trouble at the Thai military outpost, but I recalled the words of a friend in Burma, who had advised me to leave the country as soon as possible. 'You're on the blacklist because you attended the reception of astronaut John Glenn at the US Consulate. Besides that, you are teaching the Consul's two daughters at his house. They see the American car picking you up from your home. You are being watched. You're associating with capitalists and are considered a threat to this country.'

Now, even though our British passports each contained a five-dollar US note as a bribe, I feared being detained. Terror seized me and my pulse pounded with every step that brought me closer to the border. I hung onto Colin's hand.

The guard on duty read the passport and pocketed the money. We crossed the border and entered Burmese territory. *Will they let me return?*

I forgot my fear as I scoured the traders and saw the black-market goods smuggled from China and Russia. They sold at ridiculous prices far below their value, so I bought a pair of opera glasses. Fortunately, the Burmese guards at the border let me return without any fuss. On re-entering Thailand, I sank back into my seat in the tour bus and sighed in sheer relief.

The next day our bus drove to Chiang Rai. Towards dusk, we

heard the staccato sound of AK-assault rifles, and hotel guests were asked not to leave the premises during the night. Over 500 kilometres away, Burmese troops were raiding the Mae La refugee camp in Thailand, and the shots we heard were probably a skirmish between the Thai border patrol and Burmese troops returning to their HQ after the raid.

I had not realised the full danger we had been in until I read Zoya Phan's *Little Daughter: A memoir of survival in Burma and the West*. A Karen refugee, she had been in the camp at the time. Attacks on refugee camps in Thailand were apparently a common occurrence.

I thanked the Lord for my lucky escape from Burma in 1967 and again in 1998.

Chapter 12

1998–1999

A FEW MONTHS LATER, we took off for a six-week holiday to the UK. Travel not only filled us with wonder and joy, it opened our minds to how others lived and ate and died. It stoked our passions. Travel also inspired my writing and spurred me on.

We bought a Brit Rail Pass and toured England, Scotland and Wales. At Kew Gardens, I breathed in the fragrance of acres and acres of daffodils wafting towards us. Enchanted, I was reluctant to leave.

'It brings back memories of Portland, Victoria, when wandering around Daffodil Farm.' Joy lit Colin's face.

I remained silent, unwilling to break the spell.

Next, we took the train to Cornwall. The countryside was a hiker's paradise with trails that descended to isolated sandy beaches. The silence was only broken by the roar of waves or the shrill shrieks of birds.

'A penny for your thoughts,' I asked.

'I'm thinking of the time Dad and I were swept out into the ocean at Portland,' Colin replied.

I heard the tremor in his voice and wondered whether it was from sorrow at the loss of his father, or from the memory of their near-death experience. 'God spared you for me. Glad you don't live so dangerously any longer. We nearly drowned in the Heron when gale-force winds were blowing. And even though it was in Lake Burley Griffin and not in the ocean, I know what you must have felt.'

I thought of our reckless adventure on the lake and it reminded me my uncle Pat had drowned in Burma, not long after the war. His body was not found until the next day. But I pushed aside my morbid thoughts. The plaintive cries of seagulls filled the air as we gazed at the colourful fishing boats sheltering within the harbour of St Ives. According to folklore, ghosts of coastguards still patrol the area on stormy nights. Smugglers' caves beckoned.

We explored the area before setting out for Bakewell to sample their famous Bakewell pies. On the way, Colin said, 'I must stop and rest for a while. I have a dragging sensation in my groin. It's killing me.'

I was surprised, as I was usually the one wanting to rest, but thinking it had to do with his back operation, I did not worry too much.

That night, Colin was in great pain. 'It's in my lower abdomen, near my groin.'

I gave him acupuncture in the 'Pain Point.' It offered him only slight relief, but the pain eased when I pressed gently on the site of the discomfort.

The following morning, Colin was pain free, so we had some of Cornwall's famed clotted cream with our breakfast and set out on the next leg of our journey. We boarded the train to Ivybridge in Devon, a little village in the northern extremity of Dartmoor National Park. Wind whistled through hilly tussocks. The bleak conditions conjured up the deep, distant baying of the Baskerville hound. Dartmoor looked forbidding.

We hiked along in silence. Then the yapping of dogs sounded, and a dozen blood hounds dashed past. Colin paused and sat on the branch of a tree. Riders in red coats galloped in pursuit. I gasped, recalling a similar scene in the movie, *War and Peace*. 'What a thrilling sight!' I turned to Colin.

He looked pale and seemed reluctant to get up. 'The pain started but has eased now.'

'Does walking make it worse?'

'Standing brings it on, but walking is tolerable.'

'Perhaps you need to rest a bit longer?'

He stood. 'No. I'm fine now. We need to make the most of this glorious weather.'

We completed our walk, but again that night, Colin suffered an aching sensation, and I gave him the same treatment to ease his agony, wondering whether it was referred pain from his back.

Colin was fine the next morning, so we continued our train journey—on to Liverpool. The dockside stretches for seven and a half miles, and houses dozens of craft stalls. Colin was more interested in the docks. 'They are much larger than the one at Portland where I used to wander about as a child.'

I gazed around in wonder. 'In Rangoon, there were many huge ships as well as little boats called sampans. So different to this.'

We sheltered from the cold wind and peered at the Liver Building. Like watchful guardians, the two metal birds perched on top of the twin clock towers, glinting in sunlight. Buildings just across the river had been razed to the ground by the Luftwaffe during World War II, but the Liver Building still stood, bold and defiant. 'Legend says if the birds fly off, the city will cease to exist,' Colin said, a twinkle in his eye.

I elbowed him in his ribs. 'So glad the birds survived the bombing.'

He grimaced.

'How's your pain?' I asked.

'It's tolerable in the daytime,' he answered. 'As long as I rest as soon as the pain starts, I'll be right. We need to hurry.' By then, we suspected a hernia, but as it did not seem life-threatening, he carried on.

After wandering around the craft markets, we took a sightseeing cruise of the Albert, Victoria and Gladstone Docks. The Royal Albert Dock, a complex of buildings and warehouses, is the first cast iron structure built in Britain. Seaweed clung to the side of the pier, dancing to the tune of the wind whistling past and sweeping away leaves and paper in fierce gusts. Barnacles shut their mouths against the air. The swell of the water rocked the boat, and the fresh air and aroma of seaweed quickened my pulse.

'My cheeks are burning.'

'That's windburn,' Colin replied. 'It's from the cold biting wind.' The rhythm of the swaying craft and the sights and smells on the dockside brought up memories of the war. 'The Gladstone dock sheltered destroyers, sloops and corvettes of the Liverpool Escort Force, during World War Two. Remember when I read Nicholas Monserrat's *The Cruel Sea* a few years' ago? I can picture the *Compass Rose* steaming in, battle-scarred and belching smoke after skirmishes with the enemy. It's freezing here now even when we're protected from the winds. Fifty years ago, without heated cabins, the cold would have been unbearable.'

That night, Colin's pain worsened. He was in agony and I suggested seeing a doctor.

'No. If they insist on an operation, it'll ruin our holiday. I'll be laid up for the rest of the time, and what would you do all alone?'

Once Colin had made up his mind, it was always difficult to dissuade him. Besides I realised he would know when to sit or lie down to prevent a disaster.

From Liverpool, we took the train to Chester and stayed at a delightful B&B. The next morning, we journeyed by rail along the coast, so close to the sea that, at times, waves splashed us. The sun showed its face at Conway Castle as we rambled among the ruins. climbed the parapets and gazed down at the countryside. 'These ruins remind me of an old, haunted house in Portland, where I played with my childhood mates,' Colin said. 'But we should move on. Must catch the train if we want to see Hadrian's Wall.'

We hurried away and arrived just in time. The train puffed on for a few more hours to Haltwhistle, where a taxi whisked us off to Hadrian's Wall.

'It was built by the Romans to keep out the Scots,' Colin said, as we peered down from the ramparts. Cattle now grazed on the verdant pastures. 'I wonder whether the Roman guards had enjoyed the tranquillity too, or did they always have to be on the alert for the enemy?'

Colin let out a groan and flopped down on part of the ruined wall. His face was white.

'Has the pain come on? I asked needlessly.

He nodded.

I spread my raincoat on the grassy area at his feet. 'Lie down until the pain has gone.' When he had done so, I put my hand on his lower abdomen and pressed gently. *Thank God we were now at the end of our journey.*

No sooner were we back home than Colin saw our GP, Dr McKellen, who sent him to a specialist. He was immediately operated on for a double hernia. Fortunately, the operation was a success.

'You're lucky you didn't have a *strangulated* hernia,' the surgeon said, when we told him about the holiday.

'You had a double inguinal hernia which, in itself, is not necessarily dangerous, but a strangulated hernia is life-threatening and requires immediate surgery,' our GP explained later. Dr

McKellen was one of the good old-fashioned doctors, who really cared for his patients. He helped heal my distrust of all doctors.

That Christmas, five years after our get-together at my sister's place, we visited Perth again. Bertie was suffering from bouts of catatonic depression. His health had been failing ever since his minor stroke. He'd had six years of medical studies in Burma and realised he could have a more serious attack any day. I feared for his life, and recalled his words on the phone, after his stroke. 'I shall be happy if God lets me live long enough to pay for my house and leave a little nest egg for my family.'

His normally cheerful demeanour changed when Clive Junior took up smoking and drinking. Our father had drunk himself to death, and Bertie feared for his boy who frequented bars and had been enticed to try drugs. Having seen the misery our alcoholic father caused, Bertie was a teetotaller. Now, he was torn with anxiety over his son. To make matters worse, Clive had been diagnosed with a bi-polar condition. My brother's heart shattered as his son's mental health slowly deteriorated, despite the medication prescribed by specialists.

On our arrival, Bertie met us at Perth airport and drove us home for dinner. His face had aged, but his physique was the same, and he carried himself well. His son was fifteen. Young Clive was taller than either of his parents , having taken after his maternal grandfather.

We spent the next day with Rose and her family but went to midnight mass at the cathedral with Bertie and Ann. She still retained her good looks, but had put on weight. It was delightful to hear them singing in the choir again. I shut my eyes and thought of Mum, picturing us at midnight mass back in Mandalay.

On Christmas morning, Colin and I strolled along the banks of the shady Canning River with Bertie. He took us to one of his favourite haunts—the old oak tree growing not far from his home. A stab of pain shot through me. I may never again see my brother. There was no need for words now.

We stayed for three nights, knowing it may well be the last time we would be together with Bertie in this world. I was so glad we saw him before his health worsened.

Rose and Pat took us out several times and also invited us to a barbeque at their place. My younger brother, Winston, was unable to come, so we visited him at work. He was busy, but stopped long enough to return my hug. The time was worthwhile even though we could not speak much. I left, wondering how he could work in the depressing atmosphere of a mental home. Sadness passes but depression digs deep. It burrows down and remains there, dragging, suffocating and unrelenting.

We left Perth, realising we were all growing older and that some would soon be no more. *It could be me or even Colin.*

In July 1999, Colin complained of a pain in his back and leg. He had treatments by an acupuncturist and a chiropractor, but recalling his prolonged agony before his back operation, he decided not to wait too long before consulting a neurosurgeon.

'A nerve has been compressed between your third and fourth lumbar vertebrae,' the surgeon said. 'We need to operate as soon as possible.'

Despite the procedure, Colin's pain persisted until the end of August.

Feeling the need for a break, we bought tickets for several operas at the Opera House and headed for Sydney. By then we were patrons of Opera Queensland and never missed a single Brisbane performance. The joy of opera begins before the curtain rises as you await the overture, and ends long after the applause, when it echoes in your mind, enchanting you with its spells.

We enjoyed the warmth and comedy of *The Merry Widow* in the Sydney Opera House. The sets were lavish, rife with colour. It was a night to relish with its beautiful melodies, singing and dancing.

The mezza-soprano in *Il Travatore* mesmerised me with her enchanting voice. She portrayed the gypsy, whose memories had turned her into a riveting volatile central figure. I was fascinated by the singer's soaring notes, fluttering trills, seductive legato and chilling low tones. The baritone, an aristocratic but fierce Count di Luna, had a distinctive tone—rich and a trifle hollow as if he stood in an empty, echoey church. The soprano's voice was finely controlled, her tone clear and clean.

The energy of the performers in *La Bohème* amplified the physical connection between the two lovers. Their magnetism was electrifying. The soprano was a fine Mimi who imbued the character with a sense of fragility in keeping with her tragic destiny. Vocally, she was potent, the timbre of her voice rich and vibrant, hinting that Mimi remained a strong woman to the end. The baritone had an elegant sound that washed through the theatre and matched the tenor's fire, whose singing rose from one lament to another, each phrase more powerful than the previous one. At the close of the opera, he delivered his final utterance of 'Mimi!' with abandon and held on to the note for a long time.

I could not restrain my tears as the audience rose from their seats for the standing ovation. When the cheering died down, Colin and I left in a daze.

Finally, we went to *La Tosca*, a melodramatic piece set in Rome in June 1800 about a singer drawn into political turmoil. Depicting torture, murder and suicide, the composition has some of Puccini's best-known lyrical arias. The soprano was a suitably self-absorbed diva in Act I, a resourceful tigress in Act II, but a wiser woman in Act III. She held her arms forward like a Joan of Arc walking into flames with steely deliberation. The tenor's vocal lines brought out the vivid colours in his voice, and the melodramatic role he played gave his words an extra ring of truth.

After this musical feast, we left the theatre, reeling with emotion. Colin and I stepped out in silence, too thrilled to speak. I thought of Expo 88, the first time I had ever been to a live musical and marvelled at the way it had led us to opera—this pinnacle of delight.

Surprisingly, Colin had a respite from pain during those delightful days. On our return home, however, it returned with a vengeance.

'It is either due to a blood clot or an adhesion and will go away in time,' the surgeon said.

We left the surgery, angry and disappointed that nothing but drugs could ease the pain. Colin refused to take them, but the surgeon was right, and the discomfort eventually disappeared.

Not long after, Colin's eye was pierced by a thorn when be bent to look at a rose. It became infected and he was put on a course of antibiotics. I shuddered, thinking of his grandmother who had been pricked by a thorn from a rose bush and had died of blood poisoning.

By the end of the year, as if in competition with Colin, my left knee played up after a fall when hiking on the hills, and I had an arthroscopy for a torn ligament. It had been a year of pain and pleasure for us both. What would the millennium bring?

Chapter 13

2000–2003

THE 21st CENTURY COMMENCED SERENELY, despite predictions of a horrendous natural catastrophe and the arrival of the Antichrist. Colin thought of the beauty of England, of the winding roads and hedgerows with its verdant fields, and we returned in March 2000. By then, the export ban on British beef had been lifted, so we felt safe from 'mad cow disease.'

We flew from London to Dublin and took a tour of Ireland. 'The Ring of Kerry looks familiar,' Colin said. 'It reminds me of the Snowy Mountains.'

At Limerick, home of Frank McCourt, author of *Angela's Ashes* and *'Tis*, he said, 'This is like our early days in Portland when Dad worked for the Cockies. We lived in a shack with hessian walls, but my hardships were nothing compared to McCourt's.'

'Reminds me of the war. We stayed in a hut, and splinters from the bamboo floor pierced our feet.' I shuddered at the thought of those terrible times.

'Were you barefoot?'

'Couldn't afford shoes. Every cent went on food.'

We visited Blarney Castle and joined the queue of tourists to kiss the famous Stone, then off to Trinity College to see the Book of Kells. The manuscript is famous for its lavish decoration and incomparable artistry. Matthew's account of the nativity is the single most famous page in medieval art for its extraordinary fineness and delicacy.

After our visit to the college, we enjoyed a delicious dinner at the Buskers' Hotel in the famous Temple Bar. Of course, we could not leave Ireland without a tour of a whiskey distillery.

Nottingham welcomed us back with a shower of rain. Our last visit to the UK in 1998 had served to forge a stronger link with Colin's family. His cousin Paul met us at the station. His father, Uncle Clarence, thin and tall with snowy white hair, his clear blue eyes suffused by kindness, greeted us at home with his usual warmth and firm handshake. 'On your previous trip, I took you to Orlando Drive where your mother was born. Today we'll go to Sherwood Forest.'

The great oak, beneath which Robin Hood bled to death, still stands, its enormous horizontal branches propped up by beams like the crutches of an aged man.

'The tree is over one thousand four hundred years old,' Clarence said.

We caught up with the rest of our cousins before we left. Clarence organised a family gathering, where we met Paul's sister, June, and the eldest cousin Geoffrey, who was the same age as Colin.

While dining at the Magna Carta Hotel one evening, Uncle Clarence spoke to us of his work in China during World War II. 'When hostilities broke out in 1939, I registered as a conscientious objector and joined the Friends' Ambulance Unit, a Quaker organisation. I was based in the city of Kunming, in Yunnan province, near the Burmese border.'

Clarence was still a pacifist and, although over eighty years old, he and Paul worked as ministers in the Church of Christ. The epitome of kindness, he was always ready to do good for others. The more we came to know him, the more our fondness for him grew.

With regret, we said goodbye, little knowing he'd pass away in less than a year. His son Paul wrote, informing us of his death. In his email, he attached a few pages of Clarence's unfinished memoir. When I read it, I said, 'I must complete his book for him.'

I did so, and *Chocolate Soldier: Story of a Conchie* was published by Rhiza Press in 2018.

Our adventures in England took us to Matlock Bath. We walked the Limestone Trail, an excellent woodland path, then followed a steep incline to Abraham's Heights. The track took us over several stiles.

We enjoyed marvellous views and returned via the Derwent Valley Walk on the Derbyshire Downs, now a World Heritage Site. The Derwent River, Derbyshire's longest and deepest, has been harnessed to power several mills.

We drove on to Shrewsbury and stayed at a B&B. Our host served a full English breakfast on the verandah overlooking the river. It was difficult to tear ourselves away from the tranquil atmosphere, but we could not miss the Cotswolds and their honey-coloured stone cottages with steeply pitched roofs and prominent chimneys. I fell in love and felt like staying in the there forever.

Colin bought me several Lilliput Lane cottages for my collection, before we boarded a plane at Heathrow for a delightful week touring Italy. On our return, we took a tour of Dover Castle and walked through the secret wartime tunnels. Only then did we learn of their importance during hostilities. In 1940 Dover Castle's network of top-secret tunnels was the headquarters and nerve centre controlling the evacuation of Allied forces from Dunkirk. A wartime underground hospital administered urgent medical treatment to casualties from Dunkirk, as well as victims from bombing raids, before they were sent to hospitals further inland.

We returned to Brisbane in time for Verdi's *Il Travatore*, a classic Italian opera with doomed lovers, a witch, babies switched at birth, jealousy, violence and death. The plot would have been difficult to follow for those who had not attended the pre-opera talks, but the surtitles explained the dialogue. *Il Travatore* is one of Verdi's most successful operas and only exceptionally talented singers can handle its parts. The music was stirring, and we left the performance with our blood tingling, the echoes of the inspiring and uplifting *Anvil Chorus* ringing in our ears.

The next opera of the 2000 season was *Cosi Fan Tutte*, an opera *buffa* in two acts by Mozart. The story is nonsensical, but the music is sublime, brimming with duets, trios and sextets. The theme is profoundly misogynistic, but the opera is witty, amusing, and a musical delight.

Mikado, the last opera of the year, crackled with charm. It is a satire skewering Victorian England's ruling elite, and filled with catchy songs. Opera delivered so much fun and laughter that we became patrons of Opera Queensland to help develop the skills of young artists. In return we were invited to watch the first hour of opera rehearsals and also the final rehearsal.

We were not disappointed. The year 2001 treated us to three great operas—Mozart's *Magic Flute*, Verdi's *Rigoletto*, and Bizet's *Pearl Fishers*.

The year slipped by serenely until our tranquil life was disturbed by news of the deliberately lit fire at the Palace Backpackers' Hotel in Childers. We had often passed through the little Queensland country town on our way to Bundaberg, and the Palace Hotel had been a familiar sight. It had been converted to a backpackers' hostel and was a favourite with seasonal fruit pickers, 15 of whom died in the inferno. News of the fire reached every quarter of the world, as many of the dead were on a working holiday from overseas.

On September 11, shock waves rumbled across the globe when nineteen militants of al Qaeda hijacked four planes and carried out suicide attacks on the twin towers of the World Trade Centre in New York. A third plane hit the Pentagon. The hijacked American Airlines Flight 77, sliced through three light poles in the Pentagon parking lot before slamming into the first floor of the building and exploding in a fireball, instantly killing 125 people inside the Pentagon plus all 64 passengers onboard, including the five hijackers.

Passengers of the last plane, on hearing the news on their mobiles, tried to overpower their kidnappers, and the plane crashed before reaching its goal, thus sparing the Pentagon more severe damage and loss of lives.

Nearly 3000 people were killed by the tragedy. Footage of the Trade Towers collapsing played on television repeatedly. The more we watched the replay of events, the more stressed we became. Would the same thing happen in Australia? *What if the Sydney Harbour Bridge or the Opera House is blown up by terrorists?*

The 9/11 terrorist attacks caused economic damage, rippling through global financial markets. Airlines and insurance companies were the first to be hit. In Australia, Ansett Airlines collapsed on September 14.

Colin recalled the time old Reg Ansett was a bus driver and threatened to put him off because he was motion sick. We empathised with the hundreds of unpaid airline employees.

In 2002, Rose invited us again to Perth. Longing for a reunion, I accepted her offer with alacrity. On Christmas Eve, Rose and Pat met us at the airport.

The house had been decorated with a huge Xmas tree laden with gifts. It reminded me of childhood days long past, and excitement tingled through my fingers all the way up to my throat.

We all went to Mass that evening. I recalled Bing Crosby's famous words, *the family that prays together, stays together*, and drew comfort from it.

Rose had invited the whole family for Christmas dinner, but only Bertie, Ann and young Clive turned up. Winston's daughter, Tanya, came, but Winston was conspicuous by his absence. He had isolated himself from society, only going out for groceries and to the gym. I missed him terribly, but thanks to my sister we enjoyed ourselves and praised the Lord for granting us Christmas together.

The next day, Rose and Pat lent us their car to visit my friend Gem Ballantyne, a former colleague at Merici College, Victoria Square, who had helped Mum secure a teaching position when she first arrived in Australia.

That evening, Rose had a barbeque for family and friends. None of the family turned up, but I was glad to meet my sister's friends.

The following day I took the opportunity to give each member of the family either acupuncture or myothotics—a kind of massage. It gave me immense satisfaction to be able to repay my sister's generosity even in this minor way.

Rose's daughter Maureen gave us tickets to a cinema at the University of West Australia, my old alma mater, and Eileen treated us to my first-ever soccer match. I was most impressed by the cheering of the crowds. It reminded me of the tremendous enthusiasm during a bull fight in Mexico.

Drought affected most parts of Australia over much of 2002–2003, and soon became known as the 'Millennium Drought.' In January

2003, a combination of drought, high temperatures, lightning strikes and strong gusty winds caused multiple fires in Kosciuszko National Park. Wildfire moved from the Brindabella Range in New South Wales, joined two other fires, and sped towards Blundells Flat, one of our favourite haunts in the ACT. Willows, pines and poplars were burnt. The fires claimed all but one of the 19 historic arboreta, and raced towards Canberra, hitting Duffy, Rivett, Chapman and other city suburbs. Most of the huge telescope at Mt Stromlo Observatory was destroyed. Tidbinbilla Nature Reserve was not spared either. News of the fire brought back memories of our early marriage days in Canberra, and the house Colin had built for us in 101 Darwinia Terrace. One of the main reasons I had regretted leaving Canberra was because Colin had worked tirelessly on the house for over 18 months, and I had grown attached to it. My heart was crushed at the thought Colin's work would be consumed by flames.

During the fire, 488 houses were destroyed, and many others damaged, but our old home escaped. Most of the fires had been subdued by March and we breathed freely once more. The first three years of the 21st century had opened with conflagrations across Australia, but no calamity can prevent the return of spring and, with it, the prospect of better times.

Meanwhile, in February, SARS broke out in China and spread to neighbouring countries. By March, it had reached Canada. The World Health Organization issued a global health warning, and restricted travel to Asia and Canada. Fortunately, these precautions smothered the spread of the virus before it reached our shores. We sighed with relief—Australia was still the lucky country.

China and Hong Kong had suffered the most during the SARS outbreak, but the epidemic was contained by July 2003.

Our euphoria was extinguished when hostilities broke out in the Middle East. In March 2003, American and British forces invaded Iraq, leaving us in fear of another World War.

Fear is a part of life. Fear of change. Fear of the unknown. But fear compels most of us to pull back from life, whereas love opens our hearts to passion and excitement. And we were in love. When Opera Australia put on *The Mastersingers* in the winter of 2003 to mark the 190th anniversary of Wagner's birth and the 120th anniversary of his death, we flew to Sydney with members of Queensland's Wagner Society. The visit was a great success even if the weather greeted us with cold southerly winds and some light rain.

Puccini's *Madama Butterfly* was superb with a totally new set: a tranquil moat and a raised deck surrounded by rice paper walls that slid back to allow the entry of performers. Costumes gave a hint of the Orient, and the autumn scene with falling leaves in the humming chorus wakened empathy in the most hardened viewer. Petite Jennifer Barnes as Cio-Cio-San excelled herself in singing and acting; her persistent queries of the nesting times of robins, drawing tears from the ladies. The baritone, John Pringle as Sharpless, was exceptional with his voice and facial expressions.

The next evening presented us with a double bill of Rossini's farces giving added delight to the opera with its spectacular traditional setting. The music was scintillating.

The following night brought us the highlight of our trip—Wagner's *Mastersingers*. Having just heard of a lady who developed DVT after viewing the lengthy film, *The Two Towers*, we approached the theatre with some apprehension, only to find the First Act pass all too quickly. The Second Act built up to a tremendous pitch, leaving us panting for more, while the final Act bore us upwards with its crashing crescendos and spectacular costumes. Held at the Capitol Theatre with its old-world charm, it was Grand Opera at its best. Opera Australia's production of *Die Meistersinger von Nurnberg*, under the baton of Simone Young was magnificent. Wagner's musical genius worked its magic on me and for days afterward the music echoed in my ears.

The Opera House with its gleaming white sails set against the azure water of Sydney Harbour always entranced me. We took photos before entering the Concert Hall to watch *Salome*. The performance found us in the front row having an excellent view of the famed dance of the Seven Veils. Lisa Gasteen as the seductive Salome had us enthralled. We watched silent and spellbound as she cherished the bloody head of John the Baptist and kissed his lifeless lips. The trifecta of religion, sex and violence, and the Dance of the Seven Veils, elicited a visceral response from the audience and reminded me of the *Can Can* we had watched in Paris. The Dance of Seven Veils was even more seductive.

We returned home and finished Brisbane's opera season with Puccini's *Tosca* and Mozart's *Don Giovanni*.

~ Chapter 14 ~

2004

IN FEBRUARY 2004, WE FLEW to Tasmania. Our favourite walk was the one around Lake St Clair National Park, the deepest freshwater lake in Australia. I will never forget our eerie experience during our visit to Port Arthur. In one of the cells, I felt someone strangling me and, in another room, Colin saw an extra person standing with our group, so he stopped and turned to watch him, but the vision disappeared into thin air.

Praying for the dead is recommended in 2 Maccabees 12. I believe that spirits can manifest in physical bodies either because they are in pain and need our prayers, or they appear as a warning. St Thomas Aquinas explained the appearance of spirits in *Summa Theologica*, supplement, 69:3, 'According to the disposition of Divine Providence, separated souls sometimes come forth from their abode and appear to men.'

Because of our beliefs, we returned later that night, and prayed for the soul of the young inmate who had hung himself. A few minutes later, we visited the cell once more, and I was thrilled to experience a sense of peace. Perhaps all the poor distressed soul had desired was a prayer on his behalf.

The pull of Colin's homeland drew him once more. In May 2004, we returned to the UK. Our first stop was a visit to Pooh Bear's Corner in Hatfield—the first books Colin had read as a child were the tales of Christopher Robin and Pooh Bear. We drove to Salisbury Cathedral and saw the best-preserved copy of the Magna Carta. We also visited Warwick Castle, one of England's finest, and witnessed the re-enactment of a mediaeval lifestyle in the gardens. Tents were pitched in the grounds. Women sat around open fires, cooking their meal in iron pots, while children played games like hide-and-seek. Men sharpened their arrows or knives and spears while others chopped wood to keep the fires going.

We drove on to Stratford for the performance of *King Lear* by the Royal Shakespearean Company. We were so enthralled by the performance that we bought tickets for three more Shakespearean plays.

As we wanted to experience country life, we booked in at Howe's Farm in the Lake District, for two nights. The estate was set back from the road and led to a knoll on which the house stood. The neatly whitewashed two-storeyed structure was roofed with green slate from nearby Coniston. A whiff of hay and dung drifted across from the cowsheds. Black and white border collies scampered around, intent on bringing in the cows.

Colin parked our car and we strode to the guesthouse. Within minutes, the fresh-faced hostess, Lisa, appeared to escort us to our room. Colin glanced upwards at the massive ceiling beams. Then, as though the ancient structure imparted a sense of awe, he entered, careful not to hit his head on the lintel.

I rushed to the window. A path meandered through the grounds. In most parts of England, farms are criss-crossed with right-of-way tracks for hikers, and Howe Farm was no exception. 'I wonder where this pathway leads.'

Colin joined me at the window. 'Tomorrow, we'll follow the trail and find out where it'll take us.'

We rose early, in time to watch nature awake from its slumber. Mist eddied up from the lake, obscuring a tree here or a hill there, imparting a sense of peace. The lowing of cows filled the morning air. How clearly that scene remains in my memory.

The aroma of hot coffee and freshly baked bread led us to the delights of the breakfast table for a bowl of porridge laced with whiskey. We ended our meal with toast, butter and scrambled eggs, then followed the path that led us past charming cottages to Hawkeshead village.

The following morning, we visited Beatrix Potter's World where 23 story scenes from the author's books are depicted in dioramas: Peter Rabbit and Jemima Puddle-duck, Nutkin the squirrel, and many other loveable animal characters. We were the only adults unaccompanied by children, but I felt as though a fairy had waved a magic wand and I was a child once more.

After two delightful days at Howe's farm, we departed for a youth hostel at Hawkeshead—a manor set in a five-acre estate. The two-storey structure was shielded from the road by a ten-foot hedge, and in one corner of the lawn, a grove of multi-coloured rhododendrons in full bloom gave off an exquisite perfume. Fully matured oak, larch and pine recalled to my mind childhood fantasies of a hidden forest with dark trails and hideaways. The manor matched the grandeur of the garden with its Doric columns. In the foyer, grape vines painted on glass climbed all the way to the ceiling.

An avenue of trees led to High Cross Castle at Windermere. Interlacing branches of oak formed an arc above us as we entered, like a guard of honour with swords interlocked. A ridged and serrated parapet with thick stone walls and towers looked down on a carpet of buttercups spread over the lawn. A glow of warmth entered my heart as sunshine radiated its glory through the flowers.

Once settled in, we visited Dove Cottage, Grasmere, home of Britain's famous poet, Wordsworth. There he produced his greatest works and much-loved poems, including my favourite of his: *Daffodils*.

Armed with an Historic Scotland Pass, giving us free entry to castles and abbeys, we left the Lakes District. In Loch Lomond, a long and winding driveway led to the grand entrance hall of a castle converted into a Youth Hostel. As we arrived, I saw a young couple seated on a bench against the shrubbery. The girl blushed as he held her hand and sang *Loch Lomond* with gusto. This moment added to the thrill of actually being in the place made famous by the song.

After a refreshing shower, Colin went to the kitchen to prepare dinner, while I unpacked a few clothes. Once I had set up the room to look like home, I went downstairs. On the way, I met a four-foot-tall woman in a black dress and white apron, panting up the steps, carrying half a dozen cups of steaming hot tea to the top floor. I did not recall seeing her coming from the kitchen. She had unexpectedly surfaced on the stairs. Her heavy breathing told me she was straining beneath the load. I was surprised to see a housemaid in uniform at a Youth Hostel but tried not to stare at her. When we passed each other, however, I turned to watch her climb her weary way up. To my amazement, her feet barely touched the stairs. Then she disappeared as suddenly as she had appeared. *I suppose I am too drunk with happiness,* I thought.

After dinner, Colin and I set out to explore. The stairs to the first floor led to a large dining room. Above were guests' rooms. The steps creaked as we climbed to the roof of the tower, where a locked gate barred our progress. We shook the iron barrier and peered through. A sound of scampering feet answered. The odour of dust and mould hit us, and a huge black bat flapped its wings in protest. I stepped back in alarm, brushing cobwebs from my face.

Colin caught me before I fell. 'Be careful. A maid threw herself down from here. She now wanders about the building.'

I shuddered and told him of my strange experience on the stairs. 'No wonder the housemaid tossed herself down from the tower. They worked her too hard.'

'You have a lively imagination.' Colin grinned, a teasing look in his eyes.

'I saw her in daylight. I wasn't dreaming.'

I thought nothing more of it, but later Colin said, 'I too, saw the maid preparing tea in the kitchen. She worked silently, and no one else seemed to see her. Perhaps she was only visible to us.'

I suppressed a shudder and snuggled up to him. 'Hope she doesn't pay us a visit tonight.'

It may be hard to convince others, but we both know we had seen a spirit.

On our last day at the hostel, our peace was broken by a group of boisterous French students. To my surprise, they greeted me with a polite *'Bonjour madame,'* when we met on the stairway.

Before our departure, I went for a shower. The sound of loud voices assailed my ears. The students had invaded the ladies' bathrooms. They spoke without pausing for breath and sounded like the rapid fire of a machine gun.

Surrounded by a group of teenage boys, all taller than myself, I felt intimidated, but following my teacher's instinct, I pointed to the sign, *Female Toilet*. My voice rose. 'This is for women only.'

They grinned. Hot and tired, all I wanted was a shower. *Is every cubicle occupied?* I entered one with an open door. The boys stepped aside and let me pass.

Opera, Orchids and Oz

I fumed as I soaped myself but, by the time the boys had departed, I recalled that in France, I had rarely seen any segregation of sexes in public toilets. My anger soon turned to amusement.

We enjoyed many happy times at youth hostels. The accommodation was cheap, and we always cooked our own food in the communal kitchen. People were friendly and would ask the universal three questions. 'Where are you from?' 'Where are you coming in from?' and 'Where are you going?'

I will never forget the night at the youth hostel in York. There were no double rooms for couples, but we were offered a bed each, in separate dormitories—male and female. I missed Colin. This was the first hostel without a double room. Sleepless, I tossed and turned in bed. Feeling something crinkly like a wrapping from a lolly tucked in between the mattress and the bedhead, I picked it up to throw into a bin before the ants climbed into bed with me. When I switched on the light, I discovered it was a used condom.

In England, we had enjoyed pleasant walks in the New Forest, the Cotswolds and the Lakes District. In Scotland, we intended to try a more challenging hike up to the summit of Ben Nevis, Britain's highest mountain.

The peak was obscured by dark clouds when we arrived at the base. Rain pelted down in torrents and a group of weary hikers staggered towards the town, hugging their mackintoshes tight. 'They look so worn out,' Colin said. 'Are you game enough to attempt the climb?'

I sensed the challenge in his voice, and realised I was not ready for it. I wiped the rain from my face and shook my head. 'They look much younger and stronger than us.'

So we abandoned the idea of conquering the mountain, and drove on to Dumbarton Castle. We waved our Historic Scotland Pass at the man on duty and entered the castle. When we reached the topmost floor, Colin took a photo of a Scot who stood guard, in full regalia, at the entrance.

'Look!' Colin said, 'He wasn't there when we came in.'

'I hope he plays the bagpipes,' I said.

The Scot was not there when we left, and when the film was developed, he was not in the photo either. Was it another spirit? The eerie experience struck us speechless. We stared at each other in amazement.

From Dumbarton Castle, we drove to Stirling and Edinburgh Castles—the pride of Scotland. We also went to the Writers' Museum. At the sight of Sir Walter Scott's writing table, I reverently leaned forward and skimmed my hand along his desk, hoping some of his genius would pass on to me. A glow of pleasure pervaded my consciousness, as my hand skimmed over the polished surface. I have read all his books at various stages of my life. He has inspired my love for historical novels, the genre he popularised.

We proceeded to the Firth of Forth and marvelled at the long bridge across the Tay, recalling Scott's account of the collapse of this stupendous structure during a thunderstorm. We drove on, stopping at the ruins of St Andrew's Abbey and castle, exploring the deep tunnels, and satisfying our lust for history.

Our adventures took us to Melrose Abbey where Robert the Bruce's heart lay buried.

Later, we visited Scott's grave at Dryburgh Abbey. I stood in a daze before my beloved author's death mask until Colin awakened me from my trance and led me away.

Melrose, Selkirk, and Rob Roy country unfolded their beauty. I was thrilled to visit Abbotsford, Scott's home, and enter the room in which he had written his novels. The lovely garden dotted with statues of characters from his books brought him and his works to life.

We paused at Scott's View on the hills around Melrose, and read the words of his famous poem, *The Lay of the Last Minstrel*, engraved in stone. This was where his hearse stopped, as though to give the writer a final glimpse of his favourite panorama. Tears sprang to my eyes as I perused the story about his funeral.

From Melrose, we drove along St Cuthbert's Way to the Holy Island off the Northumberland Coast, crossing the causeway at low tide, the only time it is exposed. In the old days, the faithful walked the whole distance of 100 kilometres and waded in the sea to the Holy Isle. Lack of time prevented us from doing likewise, but the visit left us longing to visit sacred places like the Holy Land when the Lord had dwelt, or Lourdes and Fatima where Mary had appeared.

At York, our boots thudded on the centuries-old, cobbled streets before we headed for Nottingham. Our first stop there was Sherwood Forest, where the huge oak trees were decked in new light green leaves after the cold winter months.

Colin's cousin, June, took us to Clarence's grave and his brother Stan's crypt. A cloud of sorrow passed over us as we contemplated their last earthly resting place. But death is not the end of everything. When our time comes, we too, will enjoy the reward of eternal life in the next world, and live on in the memories of loved ones.

On our return from the cemetery, June and I climbed a ladder to their attic, to explore the contents of a box containing Clarence's letters and sermons. Like a starving child, I devoured them, knowing they would be useful when I wrote my book on his life during the war.

We left Nottingham laden with information for my writing. What an unforgettable holiday it had been.

Chapter 15

2004–2006

IN 2004, MY MANUSCRIPT, *Where's Home Mummy. A Migrant's Story*, was published. How delighted I was to hold the fruit of my labours in my hands. We made plans to launch my book in the Portland library. So in April the following year, we flew to Melbourne and saw *Il Travatore*, before going on to Portland. The opera was a new production set in Iraq during the war with Saddam Hussein. Despite the powerful vocal cast, Verdi's masterpiece was not as enjoyable as the performance in the original setting held in Brisbane, five years previously.

After a day's sightseeing and riding trams in Melbourne, we hired a car and drove to Portland where *Where's Home Mummy* was set. Colin showed me his boyhood haunts and introduced me to his friends.

My book launch was an immense success. I never expected to see such a large audience and was delighted when several of Colin's friends, as well as strangers, bought a copy.

A reporter from *The Portland Observer* interviewed me for the local newspaper.

Once back in Brisbane, I was overjoyed to have a live radio interview with Howard Ainslie of 4MBS Radio Station. Tony Tabrett, a friend from Opera Queensland, recorded it, and sent me a copy. It remains one of my fondest treasures.

After the interview, I shut down our clinic to dedicate my time to writing. I had longed to be a writer ever since I had read *Little Women,* and now my chance had come. Apart from that, the insurance for operating a clinic had shot sky-high, so it was no longer a profitable business. We dismantled the waiting room and all the consulting rooms but kept one room free for treating each other whenever necessary. Then we turned our clinic into a television room-cum-bedsitter, well ventilated on all four sides. We called it our summer cottage, but it was ideal in winter as well, because we could shut everything and turn the heaters on.

As I grew closer to my goal of being recognised as a published author, my mind flew back to Jo March who wrote about her beloved family. *Perhaps I too, could write my story?*

Before the year came to an end, the unexpected happened. My old school friend, Colleen Soord, wrote saying she would be flying out from Texas, USA, to visit her uncle Tony Rowsen in Perth. She promised to drop in to see us at Brisbane. I had first met Colleen in Mandalay soon after the war ended and the schools re-opened. We became firm friends and had corresponded over the years, but our letters ceased when I entered the novitiate, as I was only permitted to correspond with my family. We renewed our contact when I returned to secular life. I had not seen Colleen since she left Burma for the UK in the mid-forties, and now she was coming to see me. Overjoyed at the thought of meeting her again, I invited her to stay with us.

Colleen arrived on the evening of November 5. Although we had both changed in appearance, we did not take long to re-connect. We re-lived the happy times at school and marvelled at the way we had come together once more.

'We never really got to know each other before,' Colleen said, leaning towards me.

'I was so bashful and there were so many things about our lives that differed. My lack of faith, my cruel father and my restricted lifestyle.'

'Yet we were drawn to each other. I have many friends, but you are special.'

'You've always been my dearest friend,' I said.

She elicited a sense of warmth and friendship, and Colin instantly took to her.

'Where would you like to go?' I asked Colleen, the next morning at breakfast. 'Marian Valley, the Gold Coast, the National Parks or Movie World, Dream World or Sea World.'

'Marian Valley,' she replied, without hesitation. 'You've written to me so much about it. I'd love to go there.' Marian Valley, although not as famous as Lourdes and Fatima, is a place of pilgrimage for Australian Catholics.

'My son, Jason, has a friend who works in Australia Zoo,' Colleen said. 'We'll get a free entry.'

'Wow! That'll be delightful.' I looked at Colin for approval because he was the one who had to drive us out there.

Colleen loved Marian Valley. She was impressed by the devotion of pilgrims and the many shrines built by numerous nationalities to honour their patron saints. Seeing that she was so religious-minded, we also took her to the Carmelite Monastery in Ormiston for Sunday Mass. After Mass, she chatted away with the priest and nuns as though she had known them forever. That was her way—always at home with everyone.

After five marvellous days together, Colleen and I parted, richer for the renewal of a friendship that had survived the years and distance. A friend is family you choose for yourself. I felt sad to part from my life-long pal, but we made plans to visit her in Texas in the near future.

One of my dearest wishes was to go on a pilgrimage to Lourdes, so in October 2006, we flew to Lisbon and joined O'Connor Tours. A coach drove us and other pilgrims to the airport. At Fatima, we took part in the candlelight procession around the square and, the next day, we had Stations of the Cross along the path where the three visionaries, Lucia, Jacinta and Francesco used to mind their sheep. I felt inspired by the countryside where Our Lady had appeared and spoken to the three visionaries. Overcome by my feelings, I too, was drawn closer to God. Through my books, I longed to deliver the message of God's love to the world.

Leaving Portugal, we travelled through Spain and stopped at Santiago de Compostela to venerate a relic containing the remains of St James the Apostle. The Santiago Cathedral is also famous for its gigantic incense-burner. Seeing it soar nearly as high as the ceiling, is the highlight of every pilgrim's spiritual journey on the Camino de Santiago.

When the men whose job it is to swing the incensory, walked out in their red robes, an excited murmur arose among the crowd. We knew the incense burner was about to swing. The cathedral filled with smoke, and the sweet aroma surrounded us as the thurible soared to lofty heights. Its mystical charm was unparalleled. Joy filled my heart. Joy and elation. Joy and excitement.

From Santiago we went to Garabandal where Our Lady is said to have appeared. The pine needles made a green carpet at our feet and emitted a fresh fragrance. We enjoyed walking on the mountains and overcome by a renewed sense of awareness and wonder at the works of God, we felt close to the Almighty.

After a brief stay, we drove to Lourdes and participated nightly in the candlelight procession. We passed cornfields and castles, on our way to Rocamadour, which had been a stopover for Crusaders on their journey to the Holy Land. A lift carried pilgrims up to a monastery at the top, but we chose to trek to the summit. The walk is tough and portrays the sufferings of Christ. At every turn, we were confronted by a statue of the suffering Christ, but the view at the top was rewarding. It speaks of love and devotion.

Next stop was Nevers. We stayed at the Convent where Bernadette served as a nun and had the privilege of viewing her body. How fresh and lovely she looked in death, even after so many years.

Lisieux, too, had hordes of pilgrims. The pilgrimage had a lasting effect on our lives. It bonded us closer to each other and increased our prayer life. How true is the saying that the family that prays together, stays together!

On our return, we joined Teams of Our Lady, which is designed to enrich marriage spirituality and make good marriages even better. A team is comprised of five to seven couples who help each other grow closer to God and each other. It is meant for couples only. Years later, when two members brought their child along, we found it distracting and left.

Whether our lives were too full of fun and excitement, I do not know, but on the morning of Saturday 16 September, I awoke with bright red patches on my face. A prickling sensation arose when I touched them. My lip was sore. The right side of my lower lip was swollen and dotted with white spots. *Had I bitten my lip during the night?*

The doctor took some swabs and sent them off to be tested. Meanwhile, she gave me two free samples of Famvir and prescribed fungal lozenges for my white tongue and cold sores. Laboratory reports indicated an attack of shingles. The doctor told me I was fortunate to have taken the medication in time, thus preventing any further attacks. Dosed on Famvir, I lay in bed, unable to eat or even read for weeks. Sharp pains stabbed my face and ears.

On Christmas Day, the scabs on my face started to fall off. I remained weak and helpless, but we could kiss each other as the danger of contagion was over. Colin attended Mass on his own. On Boxing Day, pain wracked my teeth, ears and forehead, so I remained in bed the whole morning. As I felt better in the afternoon, Colin asked, 'Would you like to go to the Bond movie, *Casino Royale?*'

We were both fans of James Bond. I sprang out of bed and had a shower instantly.

My recovery was slow, but my appetite returned, and by the end of the year I was well enough for a swim at Hervey Bay. That evening we attended Mass in thanksgiving for all the blessings of the year and my speedy return to health. I looked forward to 2007.

Chapter 16

Farewell to Bertie, 2007

EARLY IN 2007, BERTIE'S WIFE Ann phoned to say he had suffered a stroke. We had booked a tour of India in February and were due to leave in two weeks' time. We suffered agonies, deliberating whether to cancel our trip and fly out to Perth straight away.

Within a week, Ann called to say that my brother was back home, and out of danger. So we departed on our tour. We found Delhi uncomfortably hot, steamy and congested. Perspiration streamed down our faces. We checked in at the Oberoi, in the city centre, glad to step into its cool interior with its black and white marble floor in the reception area. The hotel overlooked the 16th century garden tomb of Emperor Humayun, a UNESCO world heritage site.

The scorching inland towns are cold at night so, before retiring, Colin placed several cushions between two layers of blankets on top of us. We slept comfortably in the luxurious king-size bed with its numerous silk-covered pillows.

The gap between the rich and the poor was evident as our tour bus departed from the spotless castle grounds. The odour of cow-dung and human faeces saturated the air. We hurriedly shut the windows and saw the sights of Delhi and the India Gate, built to look like the *Arc de Triomphe*, through dust-covered glass.

Next morning, we passed several small villages, and slate and brick factories. The bus bounced and bumped its way through potholes, the degradation of the highway increasing as we travelled. Clouds of dust obscured our vision of miles and miles of mustard fields.

A roadside wedding celebration awakened our curiosity, so our tourist guide stopped the bus. The guests surrounded us, urging us to participate. Several girls dragged me into the circle of dancers, placed a turban on my head and invited me to join them. I had no idea why they had picked on me, but I tried to imitate their dance routine. They waved money at me as a token of good luck, while Colin watched with a huge grin on his face.

Hot and exhausted after the dance, we continued towards our destination—the magnificent Alsisar Mahal Hotel. A large archway led to our lounge. To the right, an *ensuite* tiled in black and white with a double shower and a dressing room hidden within an alcove. On the left, a small arch opened into an octagonal bedroom with a king-sized four-poster bed, a finely embroidered silk coverlet, cushions and pillowcases.

The sub-continent is a land of contrasts. It contains the world's highest mountain as well as sandy deserts. The tour included a camel ride across the Thar Desert. Before our camel train set out, I listened carefully to the guide's instructions, and waited until he told the camel to kneel. The most difficult part of the ride was mounting. Hanging on to the handle in front of the saddle, I put my left leg in the stirrup and threw my right leg over the hump, then settled down into the seat. When the camel rose on its back legs, I leaned back, still clinging to the handle as instructed. Then, as it raised its forelegs, I bent forward until the camel rose to its full height. I stroked its rough fur, recalling my parents' camelhair blanket. Unlike the smooth hide of a horse or cow, or the soft texture of a lamb, a camel's coat is coarse.

A camel has an odd side-to-side gait, so I let my body sway with its movements and enjoyed the ride across the sands despite the heat, the perspiration, and the odour of camel dung. The camel train went at a leisurely pace until one of the guides, obviously wanting a bit of fun, whacked my camel's rump. It took off and I bounded along, clinging to the handle and raising myself in the stirrups, as in horse riding. The wind whipped my face and sand stung my lips. I galloped on, unafraid and thrilled to the core. The guide, who rode alongside me, laughed aloud. By the signs he made to his companion, it was obvious he was commenting on my bouncing boobs.

After a while, the tour guide ordered a stop for refreshments. The camels groaned as they slowly descended to their knees. When we had dismounted, the guide handed each of us a refreshing cup of tea from a thermos and a paper bag of fresh dates. While eating, a gust of wind blew my empty paper bag away. The guide threw up his hands in horror because I was polluting the desert, so I raced down the slope into the soft sand to retrieve the offending object. I managed to grab the bag and, hearing cheers from the plateau above, I looked up to see our tourist party clapping and cheering. They seemed so far away. I had not realised the distance I'd been carried down by the sliding sand.

Feeling like a sportsman in the field, I raised both arms in triumph and hurried up the sand dune. It kept sucking me back at each step. Overcome by fear, but not wishing to admit my panic, I staggered up, only to slip back again. Two strides up and one slide down. The struggle uphill seemed to go on and on.

I worked my way up slowly and steadily, too proud to ask for help after my display of showmanship. Only when our guide, who stood on firm ground, held out his hand to help me, did I manage to extricate myself.

All the while, Colin had been watching me, not knowing my danger. I was glad because he would have raced down to save me, and we may both have been swallowed by the dune.

At the end of our ride, the camels sank to their knees, and we alighted. Seeing a bush nearby, I picked a few small branches as a treat for my camel. He chewed the leaves contentedly, but pandemonium broke out among his mates. They rose to their feet, hissing and spitting in anger. The one nearest me, drew back his lips in an ugly snarl. His teeth looked like a pair of ill-fitting dentures. He charged, hot breath steaming my face as spit flew from his snapping jaws. Only the tether rope held him back.

The camel drivers were not amused. They glared at me and rushed forward to soothe their charges. *Hope it taught them not to make rude jokes about a woman's bouncing breasts.*

The next night we stopped at Fort Khejarla, now a luxurious hotel. The stairs leading up to our rooms are a building inspector's nightmare with no rails to protect anyone from falling down the steep steps. Sure-footed in our hiking boots, we strode forward with confidence, and traversed the dangerous route to our room like mountain goats.

Ancient forts and palaces in India are now converted into hotels and we stopped at several such luxurious places. At Jodhpur, I purchased some cashmere shawls and Colin bought paintings of the Taj Mahal as well as paintings of heavily decorated elephants.

We flew out of India with one memory that stamped itself on our minds—our visit to the Kama Sutra Room. At one palace, we were left free to explore on our own but asked not to venture to the left wing. Nothing is more enticing than forbidden fruit. In a spirit of adventure, when no one was around, we threaded our way towards the prohibited rooms. Seeing a door invitingly ajar, we stepped in. There, the secrets of Kama Sutra were revealed to us. The walls had been painted with life-sized figures depicting copulating couples in various positions. It was a long time before we tore ourselves away from these revealing paintings.

By the time we flew to Perth in early September, Bertie was in hospital again. As the metropolitan hospital was full, he had been admitted into the Fremantle hospital. Because he had rallied previously, we timed our visit to coincide with the wildflower season in spring. When Bertie saw me, his chest heaved with soundless weeping. It was painful to witness his helplessness and suffering. He had lost his beautiful voice and could barely speak, yet by sheer willpower and divine intervention, he summoned up all his strength and sang Edelweiss for me.

My lips twitched in sorrow. I forced my tears back. Bertie never could bear to see me cry.

After our visit, we dropped by Winston's house, not far from the hospital. He had been suffering from depression ever since his divorce, and lived as a recluse. Still, he answered the door when we knocked, and invited us in. Overjoyed, I embraced him and tried to hide the tears that sprang to my eyes. He had hardly changed from the youth I had escorted to the airport when he had left Burma. He still had his athletic figure and the mischievous twinkle in his eyes. His home was spotless and tidy, and he had mowed his lawn within the last few days. We chatted, making up for the many years we had been apart. I thanked God for letting me see him again and felt as though I was losing one brother only to regain one who was lost and now was found.

Bertie's final days did much to bring our family together again. During our time in Perth, we drove my sister-in-law Ann and nephew Clive to Fremantle hospital so we could take photos of Bertie with his family. The following day, Sunday 16 September, we visited my sister, who had arranged a get-together with my two nieces, Maureen and Eileen, as well as their husbands, Travis and Lance. It was a bitter-sweet time.

Colin was a great support. He tried to cheer me by taking me south to look at the profusion of wildflowers. We went as far as Walpole and Cape Naturaliste, expecting a phone call urging us to hurry back because Bertie was breathing his last. Fortunately, he rallied again, and we were able to see a variety of wildflowers form a rich tapestry of colours.

When we returned from our trip south, Bertie had been transferred to a nursing home, where he would finish his days. My heart was torn to shreds to witness his sufferings, although it was a consolation to see each other before death stole him away.

Another blow hit us in July 2007, bringing us to our knees. Colin fell and struck his head on the concrete floor of our home on his way to the toilet. Half asleep, I sprang up at the sound of the thud. He lay there, unable to rise. I knew I could not help him up. He is six feet tall and, with my small stature of only five feet, it would have been impossible. I dragged a blanket off the bed and covered him, then placed a pillow beneath his head. His heart was pounding—too fast! Tachycardia!

'I must send for an ambulance,' I exclaimed.

'No, you don't,' Colin said. 'I'll be okay soon.'

I hesitated, then realised I would have to take the matter into my own hands. The ambulance arrived shortly, as our home isn't far from the Redland Hospital. The paramedics monitored Colin's heart, brought in a stretcher, then carried him to the ambulance. I locked the house and climbed into the vehicle. Colin seemed to have fallen asleep.

On our arrival, I filled in an admission form. As soon as the staff saw that we belonged to a Private Health Fund, they recommended transferring Colin to Greenslopes Hospital, which offered specialised cardiac care. The ambulance driver lost no time getting there, and after a while, Colin's heart rate stabilised. Relieved, I ordered a taxi and returned home to curl up in bed. Great sobs shook my body as I stretched out my hand to Colin's empty pillow.

I lay there and wondered whether life would ever be the same again. *Will Colin have to refrain from doing the things he loves? Will he be on heart tablets? Will he have another attack and die before help arrives?* My thoughts struggled on until merciful sleep took over...

Colin was discharged after a day. 'You must make an appointment to see me at my surgery for further tests,' the cardiologist insisted before we left.

His words did nothing to reassure me.

When Colin underwent the stress test a few days later, the surgeon said, 'You're disgustingly fit. Go home and continue whatever you're doing. There's nothing I can do for you.'

What a relief to hear those words! The tachycardia had occurred because Colin's blood pressure had dropped when he got out of bed too suddenly. We went home, thanking God for saving Colin. We realised how precious and fragile life is. Like a camel, life can go forward but cannot go back.

Chapter 17

2008–2009

ONE AFTERNOON IN MARCH 2008, Colin and I gazed at the invitation from Government House, Queensland. The top of the card was embossed by a golden crown—symbol of Her Majesty, Queen Elizabeth. Dazzled by the gold that glittered in the rays of the sun, we read:

Her Excellency the Governor and Mr Michael Bryce AM AE
Invite
Mr and Mrs C.R. Barker
To a reception
Wednesday, 16 April at 6.00 pm
Government House Fernberg Road Paddington

RSVP 9 April 2008
Lounge suit/ Cocktail Dress

'How did they hear of us?' I asked Colin.
'We're patrons of Opera Queensland. Someone must have given them our names.'
We sent in our acceptance straight away.

On the evening of the reception, we drove to Government House and parked in the grounds, which consisted of a formal garden and natural bushland. Paths meandered through the area.

We were ushered into the central foyer, which had a large fireplace. An intricately carved timber staircase overshadowed a large stained-glass window depicting a life-size Robert the Bruce. In the formal reception room on the ground level, we were served wine and hors d'oeuvre. After being presented to Her Excellency Ms. Quentin Bryce, AC, the governor of Queensland, we took our seats for the Queensland Orchestra Young Artist Recital and were handed a programme of the performance.

The audience was treated to arias from *Carmen, The Marriage of Figaro, La Bohème, Cosi Fan Tutte* and so many others. I was thrilled by the music, the rich voices of the singers and the elaborate setting. Every so often, my eyes alighted on the string of pearls adorning the governor's neck. Colin had given me a similar set as an engagement gift in 1970. I squeezed his hand. He glanced at me and returned my gesture.

We had been patrons of Opera Queensland for ten years and enjoyed its privileges with its cocktails at Southbank, celebrity afternoon teas, invitations to dress rehearsals, and complimentary tickets to movies. The invitation to Government House in 2008, however, had been the highlight of our time as opera patrons.

The year continued with the performance of *The Barber of Seville* and *The Magic Flute* and ended with the launch of the 2009 season performances, and the patrons' Christmas party.

Bertie remained in a nursing home for over a year and passed away peacefully in June 2008.

Rose phoned me the night before he died. 'He will not last the night. Don't mention it to anyone.'

I was grateful to her for imparting the dreadful news. Mum used to say, 'Always pray for a happy death.' I realised that death would come to all of us sooner or later and prayed for Bertie more intensely than ever.

He appeared to me that night. He floated above the foot of our bed and looked down with a joyful, uplifting smile. He was happy and handsome, as he had been in his youth. All his sufferings had vanished. He had gone to meet his Maker and reap the reward of a good life.

I am forever grateful to Bertie for having given up his job to help us get away from our cruel father. He had sponsored us all out to the UK and had been a loving and protective brother.

As always, Colin empathised with my loss and did his best to comfort me.

Rose's daughters Maureen and Eileen celebrated two red-letter days in 2008. Eileen announced her engagement to Lance Mitchell early in January. In October, Maureen completed her studies in Law, and was awarded a degree as a fully qualified lawyer.

Rose emailed to inform me she and Pat would be flying to Brisbane in October. My sister sometimes visited us on the way to or from an overseas destination. This time, however, she and Pat were coming for a week's holiday.

We met them at the airport and brought them home in time for breakfast. Rose gave me a souvenir from Cappadocia—a miniature of the caves—and a little round musical box from Vienna. It had a gold-rimmed cover and a hand-painted Austrian crest on white marble, played a popular Viennese tune. Souvenirs from my sister's overseas holidays are all over our home. They stand in glass cabinets among those from our own travels; welcome reminders of her.

'Choose the places you wish to visit. This is your holiday and I want you to enjoy yourself,' I said.

'Noosa and Byron Bay,' she said. 'We saw them on television and mean to book tours to those areas.'

'Don't do that. We'll take you there,' Colin offered.

Rose's eyes lit up, and my heart lifted to see her joyful smile. All too often, she smiled a sad smile—just like Mum's.

On Sunday 17, we set off for Noosa and stopped at Mt Coo-tha Lookout. When we were alone, Rose blurted out, 'Let's be friends.'

Over the years, Rose had often confided her troubles to me, and I felt the urge to protect her as I had done when she was a child. However a love-hate relationship had developed between us. Neither of us could see eye-to-eye in many things. I resented her lack of understanding, yet loved her because we had been through so much together. We had many personality clashes. Although I had boiled within, I never retaliated. When Rose angered me by saying hurtful things, I recalled my father using cruel words to Mum and beating her up. Next morning, he would kiss her and ask for forgiveness. I saw him in my sister and steeled my heart against her.

Now, instead of accepting her offer of peace, I recalled all the times she had accused me of deceit and hypocrisy, and I could not find it in my heart to forgive her. 'All I want is peace. You'll always say hurtful things.'

Looking back now, I should have hugged her and forgotten past injuries. Unfortunately, an unforgiving nature is my greatest failing.

We both dropped the matter and continued as if nothing had been said. Later, I came to regret my words. But what is said cannot be unsaid. I am willing to ask her to forgive me, but will she reject me in turn? Perhaps someday I will apologise, even if it is on my death bed. May God forgive me for what I have done.

Colin stopped at Aussie World to show Rose and Pat the Ettamogah Pub. 'The timber building, sloping walls and a distinct architectural style is like the famous cartoon pub. In the old days, the cartoon was a familiar sight in the *Australian Post*, but the magazine is out of circulation now.'

After a short stay and lots of photos, we continued our trip to Noosa. Rose was fascinated by the renowned tourist haven and insisted on treating us to dinner.

On the first day of their arrival, I had given Rose my manuscript to peruse in case there was anything in it she might object to. She had been reading it at nights, but had not yet finished.

'Keep it with you until you leave for Perth,' I said, while she was packing her things.

On their final day, we picked up Rose and Pat from their hotel and drove to Byron Bay. A rush of sadness overcame me as us we wandered up to the lighthouse to revel in the view and take photos. I wondered when I would see them again. She was my sister and I loved her despite her occasional harsh words.

That evening, we took them for dinner at the Irish Club. Pat was filled with enthusiasm and chatted away with the manager. That day remains etched in our memories, not only because of our time together, but because the famous club was sold a few years later in 2015. Tara House in Elizabeth Street, pride of the Irish in Brisbane for nearly a hundred years, is an Irish Club no longer.

On the day of their departure, Mum's sad smile flickered on Rose's face as we waved goodbye. A spasm of sorrow pierced me.

On 10 October 2008, a few days after my sister and her husband had returned to Perth, the Sydney Morning Herald reported: 'Australian shares suffered their worst day since the crash of 1897, losing more than 8%, as mounting recession fears sent equity markets tumbling around the world… BHP Billiton shaved the most off the index,

falling $2.10, or 7%, to $27.74, Rio Tinto fell $5.01, or 6.4% to $73.00... Banks accounted for much of the main index's fall, given their relatively steep falls and size.'

Colin had predicted a crash in the share market and taken precautionary measures, yet my hand trembled on reading the news. 'Do we still own shares in BHP and in the banks?'

'Sold all our BHP shares at a loss before they hit bottom.' A hint of triumph edged his voice. 'But I've held on to the bank shares. They pay good dividends, and we can hang on to them until they rise again.'

We checked our portfolio once more and sold the rest of our shares, even though they went at a loss.

When Lehman Brothers, the American investment bank, filed for bankruptcy, the world's financial markets experienced a full-blown crisis. By March 2009, the FTSE fell by another 1500 points to just above 3500. We thanked the Lord we had never used margin loans. Neither did we face a huge loss or lose our home when the market fell. Our savings dwindled, however, and we were forced to cut back our expenditure.

Having already booked and paid a deposit on a holiday to New Zealand in February, as well as another big tour of Europe in September/October, we intended to travel overseas while still in a position to do so. We flew to Auckland to visit my maternal granduncle's widow, Fairy Scriven. I'd exchanged a few letters with my granduncle who had died a few years earlier, but it was good to see someone Mum had spoken about when I was a child.

We enjoyed the thermal baths at Rotorua. At Wai-O-Tapu, the Thermal Wonderland was a sensory feast of coloured sands, white alum cliffs, the smell of sulphur, the constant bubbling of hot mud and the laughter of children.

In early February 2009, a period of drought, high winds and soaring temperatures caused bush fires all over Victoria. Our favourite camping ground at Halls Gap in the Grampians was threatened. I had first sighted a koala in the wild at Halls Gap. Now, I shuddered at the sight of scorched and sick koalas shown on television. The worst day of the fires will always be remembered as Black Saturday.

We flew to Perth in May 2009 for Eileen's wedding. The grand reception featured excellent wine and scrumptious food. Eileen was a picture of joy. Rose thought she looked very much like Catherine Zeta-Jones, a name I did not recognise.

Maureen, who was a year older than Eileen, was tall and willowy. She walked gracefully and radiated confidence. She had married a few years earlier, but we had been unable to attend her wedding. It was lovely to see the two sisters dressed in their finery. Rose had spent a small fortune, but she loved her children and wanted the best for them.

We went on our final European tour in September and October 2009 with Odyssey Travel, the most expensive and luxurious tour we ever experienced. During our stopover at Dubai, Colin bought me two bottles of rose essence—my favourite perfume.

In Germany, we visited the Hohenschwangau and Neuschwanstein Castles, and Colin presented me with two miniatures of them as souvenirs. Being opera lovers, we appreciated the visit to Ludwig II's Linderhof Castle and the Venus grotto. At Salzburg we visited the Mozart Museum and later, we went to *The Magic Flute,* performed by puppets. We so enjoyed it, we came home with a DVD of the opera.

Our guide dropped us off at the Obersalezberg Documentation Centre, a permanent exhibition near Berchtesgaden, before taking us on a tour of Hitler's Eagle's Nest. The Berchtesgaden area had been one of Hitler's favourite retreats. Nazi top dogs had their recreational residences there also. Barracks and bunkers for the SS were built nearby and it soon became a significant Nazi headquarters.

Colin and I looked out from the open-air terrace outside the centre and saw the peak of the Kehistein mountain and the Eagle's Nest tea house perched on it. The main attraction for tourists are the tunnels and bunker system. We were permitted to explore them via a walkway circuit. We peeked into the dead end of tunnels where the rock had been hewn out of the mountain by weak and starving prisoners-of-war until they literally dropped dead. We came to a deep abyss said to be 30 metres deep. An eerie feeling crept up my back as I gazed into its depths, so I reached out to grasp Colin's hand, but he was no longer with me. Other tourists, too, had left. Realising I was alone in the most sinister part of the tunnels, I turned cold and hurriedly retraced my path through the dark maze. My breathing ragged, my pulse racing, I stumbled along until I caught a glimpse of light in the distance. Colin stood, silhouetted against the blinding ray of sunlight.

I grasped his hand. 'Why did you leave me alone?

'It was too oppressive in there. A strange sensation crept over me. I heard the cries of men under interrogation and sensed their suffering. It was unbearable. I just *had* to leave.'

I opened my mouth, yet the words, 'But you left me alone!' froze on my lips. I saw his pale face and felt his icy hand. 'Let's get out of here,' I said.

We clambered back on the bus, where the other passengers sat waiting for us.

The 'Eagle's Nest' is over 1834 metres high and rises above the town of Berchtesgaden. It is called the Kehlesteinhaus in German, after the Kehlstein mountain on which it stands. It was built in only 13 months by forced labour. A large gleaming brass elevator took us to the top of the mountain, directly above Hitler's summer home, the Berghof. It was there the famous photographs of Hitler relaxing in the summer with Eva Braun and his dog were all taken—not at Eagle's Nest. Hitler did not go there often because of his fear of heights.

At Kehlesteinhaus a fireplace of red Italian marble dominates the reception area—once the Nazi Conference Room. The stone walls are as solid as a castle to serve as protection from enemy bombs. A small side room a few steps down used to be Eva Braun's tea room, where she would entertain state visitors or diplomats' wives, while the men next door discussed politics and war, and hatched their murderous plans. The infamous tea house was built for Adolph Hitler's 50th birthday. It is now a beer garden and a tourist restaurant. There is also a shop selling Eagle's Nest T-shirts, postcards and brochures, DVDs and books.

We were fortunate to get a panoramic view of the valley below before it was shrouded in mist. The scenery was heavenly. While exploring the underground bunkers, chills had run down my spine as I thought of the countless infernal acts of sadism carried out there. The contrast between the peaceful scenery above and the gruesome feelings we experienced in the tunnels brought home the difference between heaven and hell as it had never done before.

The following day we drove through the Julian Alps and stopped at the shores of Lake Bled. A boat took us to the island. The lake was calm at first but later a breeze came up, shattering the surface of the water into shards of light. Back at the village of Lake Bled, we bought hot roasted chestnuts and reminisced about our trip to London in 1980, when we had first tasted these delights on a cold, crisp December night.

The next morning, we left for Ljubljana and took a funicular up to the castle. The following day, we set out for Opatija in Croatia to visit the 24-mile-long heritage-listed Postojna Caves. We boarded an electric train at the entrance, and went through a web of tunnels, passages and galleries into the famous underground kingdom. I gasped at the beauty and magnificence of this natural wonder.

Colin bought me a turquoise necklace and matching earrings as well as several miniature houses in Croatia. We toured the Istrian Peninsula, which jutted out into the Adriatic Sea, and saw couples walking hand-in-hand while soft music drifted from nearby hotels. The area cast a spell on Colin. He was reluctant to leave Opatija, but our coach was departing for Italy the next morning.

On our arrival at Castelbrando, a guide took us for a tour of the castle. On the final day of our holiday, I said, 'All my youthful castles in the air have now been realised. My Prince Charming has rescued me, and we have flown away on our magic carpet. I now realise that my childhood of chaos was meant to steer me to Australia.'

'And lead to the blossoming of a full life with travel and opera,' Colin added.

Happy and content, we flew home. Drawn to the same sights and sounds during our trips, our travels brought us even closer to each other than before. Colin held me in his arms and kissed me. His mild tenor voice turned thick and hoarse. Hoarse with passion. There was no need for words.

We realised this was possibly our last trip to Europe, but there would be other adventures nearer home. Money was meant to serve, not to rule us. We had risen above our financial problems.

Chapter 18

Milestones & Mishaps, 2010

2010 IS REMEMBERED AS THE beginning of a decade of drought, fires and floods. For us, it marked the end of our patronage of Opera Queensland, and the commencement of Colin's woodworking.

Colin had been looking for a hobby ever since his retirement and, now that share trading did not take up his time, his search intensified. He bought a lathe, some rare and exotic timber, and tried making bowls, boxes and pens. He also constructed a red mahogany chest of drawers that came in very handy for storing our winter woollies and excess clothing. Delighted with the result, we stood it against the end of the passage wall, with a mirror above, for visitors to view themselves when leaving the bathroom.

On January 6, when I rang Winston for his birthday, he did not reply. He had once warned me he possessed a Doctor Jekyll and Mr Hyde personality, and when in Hyde mode, he never answered the phone. So, the following day, I rang again, hoping he was in Jekyll mode. This time, he answered my call, and we chatted for a long time. He always spoke cheerfully despite his frequent bouts of migraines and depression.

In February, on our 41st wedding anniversary, Colin and I drove to Burleigh Heads National Park, 90 km south of Brisbane. Parking our car near Goodwin Terrace, we began our walk on the Lookout Trail. Pandanus palms clung to the rocky surface; the wind whipped up and we hung on to our Akubras, scanning the sea for migrating whales. The briny smell enervated us, and we walked briskly along the path until we reached the turn off to the Rainforest Track up the mountain.

Wind rustled the sun-dappled leaves of the forest red gum, the brush box, and the grey ironbark. We enjoyed the complete change of scenery and the cool atmosphere. As we ascended the hill, we caught glimpses of the rolling waves crashing on the rocks below, threatening to smash the surfers. At times, we passed bare rockfaces where erosion had caused landslides. Seeing a sign, 'Beware of falling rocks,' we hastened our steps until we paused at a lookout for a good view of the steep cliffs below.

The headland is eighty metres in height, and the walk ends down a flight of steep stone steps. Before descending, we gazed in awe at the angry waves dashing against the rocks below. We had often done this walk, but the view never failed to delight us. This time, however, my boot caught on a fissure and I lost my balance. I teetered on the brink of the steps before flying through space, head foremost. As luck would have it, I was able to grab a sapling beside the track. The small but sturdy tree stopped my flight, but the momentum carried me forward, and my legs swung out. I hung on grimly and landed safely on my feet. I sat on the steps for a few minutes to recover my breath, while Colin ran down to check on me. He always let me set the pace, because of my difficulty in matching his lengthy strides. So he had been too far behind to steady me. We lay beneath the shade of a tree to slow my pulse before having a swim.

We ended the day with a delicious Japanese meal at Broadbeach, grateful for life's blessings. It was late by the time we drove home. Out of the darkness, a wallaby sprang forward like a suicidal maniac, too late for Colin to hit the brakes. We stopped, dragged the poor dead animal from the road and inspected our Volvo for damage. The car seemed unharmed, so we drove on until a warning light indicated empty car coolant.

'The radiator must be damaged,' Colin said. 'But we're not far from home. We'll keep driving. Hope we make it.'

The next morning, we drove to a garage but had to stop every two minutes to fill the leaky radiator. We returned home a few hours later, a thousand dollars poorer.

The following day, an old friend, Marie Lazaro, phoned to say that she and her daughter Brenda were staying at the Rendezvous Hotel in Brisbane. I had first met Marie when Mum had fled from my father and taken refuge with us in a convent. The nuns had given us two rooms in their home for the aged. Mum and my two infant brothers stayed in one room, Rose and I were next door.

The convent had an orphanage, and Marie was one of the senior girls who looked after the orphans. She had fascinated me with stories of life in Mandalay during the Japanese occupation. 'Japanese forced the nuns to send the senior girls to nurse wounded soldiers, in their military hospital. Being the youngest girl, I'd been given the job of tea-lady for the patients. Japanese stored caskets containing body parts in the hospital, before shipping them to Japan. It was horrible. I was made to bow each time I walked past the caskets on my way to serve tea. At nights, I dreamed of the corpses coming to life and doing a ghoulish dance.'

I would listen in horror to her tales but, after I left to join a novitiate, I lost touch with Marie. She was now a widow, but her daughter took care of her and accompanied her everywhere. They lived in Queanbeyan on the ACT border and were having a holiday in Queensland.

We brought them home and, over a cup of coffee and a chat, asked if they wished to go anywhere in particular. 'The Warehouse Outlet—the DFO,' they both said.

After shopping, we took Marie and Brenda out for dinner before dropping them off at their hotel.

I had been suffering from aches and pains since my fall, so the next day we went to our chiropractor. He set everything right, and we returned home, looking forward to having an afternoon nap. Within a few minutes, Colin's cousin, Terry, phoned to say they had arrived from Melbourne, and that their stay would be short, as they had been in Melbourne, catching up with old friends from the UK.

We offered to put them up, but they chose to stay at a hotel. We picked up Terry and his Welsh wife, Inga, brought them to our house, and spent the rest of the morning exchanging notes on family histories.

For ten years we had been patrons of Opera Queensland, donating a thousand dollars each year towards the company. We lived gloriously, and tasted life to the full. Our days had been filled with music and travel, but with the collapse of the stock market, it was time to start budgeting for the future. We decided to withdraw our patronage, but still remain in the Queensland Opera Club for a small fee of twenty-five dollars annually. We also limited our travels to closer destinations like Singapore or Hong Kong. When we could no longer survive on our capital, we intended to apply for a pension. We had enjoyed the luxury of wealth for a while, but were grateful to still have our health, and could look forward to a comfortable old age.

We made the most of our last year as patrons and went to cocktail parties and rehearsals as well as their public performances. My favourite opera that year was *The Merry Widow*, with its beautiful waltzes, romance and happy ending. Not a tragic ending like most operas.

Opera, Orchids and Oz

Before the year ended, we attended our final cocktail party at Opera Queensland.

In August, the breath of spring was in the air, and the volatile oils of the wattle spread their invigorating fragrance. Life went on smoothly until Rose phoned to say Pat was to be operated on for a malignant melanoma. C.A.N.C.E.R. The word conveyed dreadful connotations. My heart ached for my sister. I would be out of my mind if Colin were ever diagnosed with it.

Three weeks' later, Rose phoned to say Pat's tonsils had been removed, but no cancer cells had been present. *What a relief the cancer had not spread! Detection and treatment work are painful for the victim and heartbreaking for the family.*

Another week went by. Then Rose said that Pat may be having chemotherapy.

I shuddered. *If only we lived in Perth, we could take turns to drive him to hospital for treatment.* 'So sorry we're too far away to help.'

The next day, my sister spoke excitedly on the phone. 'Pat won't be having chemo after all. The oncologist has decided to give him radiation instead.'

'That's a relief,' I said. *'Deo gratias!'*

In September, while Pat was recuperating from his successful operation, Rose and Eileen left for a pilgrimage to the Holy Land. *What better place to pray for his recovery than where Jesus trod?*

On her return, Rose sent me a colourful bag from Israel. At the same time, Inga's DVD of *The Loneliness of the Long-Distance Runner* arrived by post. I loved the bag, and Colin and I enjoyed the DVD which was based on the true story of a Nottingham boy.

September ushered in the Queensland Writers' Festival. I had come to appreciate the benefit of critical appraisal for my work and had joined a number of writing groups—Carindale Writers', Ruff Writers, Gold Coast Writers' as well as the Vineyards Group.

Full of excitement at the thought of hearing famous authors speaking about their books, I looked forward to the festival. On the first day, I wore my turquoise necklace, a memento of our trip to Croatia, and a gift from Colin.

On my return home, the necklace was missing. I bit my lip and searched everywhere. I prayed. I emailed the library. Nothing. I recalled the time I had lost my gold chain in the shower, while camping in the Grampians. It had been a parting gift from Mum before she left Burma for the UK and I had been heart-broken at its loss. I had prayed for its recovery, and my precious chain had been handed in to the receptionist.

Once again, I prayed, hoping someone would return it. A few days later, I went to the library. 'Has anything turned up?'

The receptionist passed me an envelope. In it was my beautiful blue necklace. Her eyes sparkled. 'Someone found it on the floor in the toilets.'

Ever so grateful, I offered a reward for the finder.

The receptionist shook her head. 'It was handed in anonymously.'

Not long after, Colin and I went for our annual check-up at the optometrist and were told we had cataracts. I also had glaucoma.

Colin needed an operation on his left eye urgently, so he had it on 31 March. Two weeks later, the surgeon declared his vision in that eye 20/20. As for me, the eyedrops prescribed for glaucoma gave me asthma-like symptoms—coughing and shortness of breath—so I stopped using them.

My sight continued to deteriorate and was particularly poor at nights. One Friday evening, 13 August, after the Vineyards Writers' Group meeting, I went to the carpark to meet Colin. The lights were off. Unable to see in the dark, I stumbled, tripped over the retaining wall, and fell to the lower level, striking my head on the brick wall. Fortunately, I landed on the shrubbery, which broke my fall and spared my bones.

I lay there looking at the stars. *How beautiful they are!* I felt myself drifting off to sleep. In my semi-conscious state, an inner voice told me to get up. A breeze blew a soft breath of air and revived me. I rose slowly and, with outstretched arms, threaded my way towards where I thought our car would be.

'What are you doing here?' A voice broke the silence. A voice so comforting, I could have sobbed from joy. I recognised a friend from the writing group.

'I had a fall. I can't see much. I'm looking for our car. For Colin.'

'I'll take you to him.' Knowing my eyesight was poor, she led me to our car.

When I told Colin of my accident, he grabbed his torch out of the car and we checked where the accident had occurred. It was quite a height.

He held me in his arms. 'You're fortunate not to have broken any bones.'

My eyes continued to worsen, and the pressure flew up to 19/20. The ophthalmologist said he wanted to bring it down to 7/8 and put me on different eye drops, but they gave me the same asthma symptoms as the previous ones. When I mentioned it to the specialist, he said he would put me on some drugs to alleviate the asthma. I checked up on them and discovered they could cause liver and kidney problems. I had to choose between being blind and healthy or dying from liver disease or kidney failure. As a naturopath and acupuncturist, I chose to have a healthy life at the cost of my sight and refused to use the eye drops. I went to an optometrist for a new pair of glasses as the old pair was now practically useless.

He gave me a Field Vision Test. 'Your right eye has deteriorated, and you have lost part of your peripheral vision. You must use your drops, or you'll go blind!'

I wondered how I would cope with pouring boiling water into a teacup or cutting up meat and vegetables for dinner. At nights, I dreamed of falling into a ditch, getting run over by a car or walking into a tree. During the day, I thought of how I would miss the lovely scenery, the Christmas lights, and above all, I'd never again see Colin's dear face or even myself in a mirror. I dreaded the thought of awaking each morning to a dark day. My days would be filled with darkness. Darkness would envelop me. Darkness would take possession of my soul.

I prayed for a cure and waited for an answer. Then it came. I would still feel the warmth of the sun, the warmth of Colin's presence. The warmth of his arms around me. The warmth of his body. I would hear his voice, the singing of birds, the sound of music, and the voices of my friends. God's voice would not cease to speak to me.

I loved to read. I could borrow audio books from the library. I could still write. There were ways of having my words down via computer programmes. My books could still be published. I resigned myself to the inevitable.

Colin would not give up so easily. He suggested seeing another eye specialist and scoured the Yellow Pages until he came across an ophthalmologist who specialised in glaucoma. The surgeon recommended a trabeculectomy to relieve the pressure on my eyes.

'I'll bore a hole to drain the excess liquid from your eyes, and also remove your cataracts at the same time.'

I decided to go ahead as soon as possible. The operation was a success, but I felt weak and faint for some days afterwards. My second eye was operated on, the following month.

I recovered quickly but found myself unable to keep my commitments, so at the end of June, I resigned from the Vineyards

Writing Group. Now I go for regular Field Vision tests to check for any further deterioration. My eye pressure has stabilised, and I do not need to use eye drops for glaucoma.

From this, I learned to trust in God and never give up.

Rose rang to inquire after the results of the operation and informed me she would be retiring in September. 'I've bought Pat a new car, a Great Wall 4-wheel drive.' She sounded happy. I was glad she was stopping work. Psychiatric nursing was not an easy job—and night shifts are bad for health.

We flew to Hong Kong in December, as we wanted to visit the sites of the battles during World War II and the war cemetery in case my sight deteriorated any further. We were not disappointed. On Christmas Eve, carol singers stood on every street corner. The decorations were spectacular. Christmas trees sprouted in every square and prominent areas. At church we were regaled by welcoming smiles of devout worshippers and all the traditional carols.

Boxing Day found us in Disneyland, Hong Kong. We had been to Disneyland in California years ago and recalled the thrills, the Disney characters, the parades. Now we rejoiced to see our old favourites once again. What a delightful place Hong Kong was. One did not have to travel all the way to America to visit Disneyland and enjoy all the Christmas festivities at the same time.

So, 2010 ended on a happy note.

Chapter 19

2011

WE BROUGHT IN 2011 WATCHING THE fireworks in Hongkong and spent the day at Stanley Beach, having a last-minute shopping spree. We flew home on 3 January. During our absence, Queensland had been hit by a series of floods. The Brisbane River broke its banks, severely affecting suburbs along the river. We feared the creek beside us would rise and reach our home, so Colin worked frantically in the rain, diverting the water towards the storm drains. Fortunately, the creek did not overflow.

Cyclone Yasi struck Mission Beach on 3 February, inundating properties around Tully and Innisfail. I recalled the cassowaries we had seen at Mission Beach, the wildlife, the cattle and sheep—my heart went out to all those in distress.

Further south, a wild thunderstorm unleashed its deadly power on the Lockyer Valley. Residents in Grantham clambered on their rooftops, awaiting rescue, while watching trees, vehicles and people sweeping past. I thought of those who lost their property, animals and lives and, recollecting how we had felt at our losses during the war, I empathised with them. Everyone from our street banded together and held a garage sale to raise money for the flood victims.

Because our Volvo's brakes still gave us endless trouble, Colin took the car in for a check-up. 'The red lights always indicate that the ABS brakes are not working.'

The mechanic peered beneath the bonnet of the car and looked bemused. Everything seemed in order. He leaned forward and nodded. 'Um… computer…'

Colin hated computers. He recalled the days he repaired his own cars and rarely took them in for repairs. 'Why can't we just tear out the computer and fix the car without it?'

The mechanic held up hands, palm outward and backed away. 'No! No! You can't do that.'

'What can you do?' Colin's voice rose.

The mechanic scratched his head. 'It's difficult to obtain parts for it. We'll have to order them from overseas.'

'We invested in a Volvo because they are reputed to be safe and supposed to last forever!' Colin said.

Frustrated, we wondered why we had spent so much on a brand-new car. The Volvo remained in the mechanic's garage, so we dipped into our savings and hired a car to take us places. Then we applied to Centrelink for a pension. It would take months to be approved.

To celebrate our Ruby Anniversary, Colin bought me a pair of heart-shaped earrings studded with rubies, along with a ruby pendant. Then, after dabbling in family history, woodwork and growing roses, he decided to try his hand at orchids. He set about constructing a shade house for his collection.

In September, Rose and Pat went for a holiday to the USA. On their return, Rose invited us to join them in Busselton the following April. She said she would rent a chalet for the four of us for a week.

Surprised by this unexpected invitation, I exclaimed, 'The

wildflowers won't be out!' I knew that the best time to visit was in the spring. The cost of flying over for a week in autumn would be more than we cared to spend for a brief time together.

I think Rose was annoyed with me for declining her invitation. Perhaps she thought I was more interested in the wildflowers than family. However, Perth was a long way to go for such a short holiday, and it would be wet, windy and cold at that time of the year.

Meanwhile, Winston withdrew into himself and would not answer phone calls from either of us. I guessed his depression had grown worse, and was sad for him, but was too far away to help. Even Rose, a psychiatric nurse, could do nothing for him. His work gave him a dread of drugs and hospitalisation. He stayed away from doctors and refused to have any treatment for his depression. All I could do was to pray for my family.

We went to only two opera performances in 2011. We had seen them previously, but by different musical directors. They were excellent—*Cosi Fan Tutte* by Mozart, and *Tosca* by Puccini. *Cosi Fan Tutte* is Mozart's most controversial opera for his satirical take on relationships between men and women. Loosely translated, the title means 'women are all like that'. We shook with laughter at the lively humour and enjoyed the uplifting music.

Tosca is Puccini's operatic thriller set in Napoleonic Rome, and the electrifying scores feature some of his most memorable melodies. I left the theatre with tears in my eyes at the tragic ending.

Colin and I celebrated Christmas with a traditional roast duck and plum pudding, ending the year by attending a Thanksgiving Mass at Marian Valley. Please God, let 2012 be less stressful, I prayed. I realised things could have turned out much worse than they did. Our home had not been flooded, our Volvo brakes had not broken down when we were driving in the mountains, stranding us or causing an accident.

What an eventful year it had been.

Chapter 20

When One Door Closes, Another Opens, 2012

2012 COMMENCED WITH A BANG. Our friends, Jim and Barbara Phillips, took us to a club over the border at Tweed Heads, and we danced late into the night. We enjoyed bringing in the New Year with friends and returned home, drunk with happiness.

Colin was now in two woodwork clubs. He attended classes and excelled in making pens from exotic timber. He sent them to his English cousins, who marvelled at the beautiful wood and excellent craftsmanship. My friend, Colleen, was also overjoyed by his gift and informed us her fellow Americans were crazy about them. Another friend, Carole, who had just been back from a trip to the US, confirmed this by saying someone had asked her for one.

In April 2012, we went to New Zealand for a ten-day holiday. Hiring a car, we drove to Queenstown and Arrowtown in the South Island and were charmed by their autumn colours. New Zealand is a miniature Europe with all the beauty of that continent including fiords, mountains and glaciers, as well as fine food. Colin and I particularly loved the delicious blue cod and the venison. *How fortunate we are to live not too far from such a beautiful land!*

We booked a pilgrimage with Harvest Tours to visit Rome, Assisi, Monte Casino and other religious places in Italy. The trip had been scheduled for September but, in July, Harvest Tours informed us the tour was cancelled due to a lack of bookings.

It was all for the best because we were struck down by 'flu in August and incapacitated for ten days. The road to recovery was long and tedious. Only later did we discover that we had an allergic reaction to some preservatives and flavourings in the rissoles from our butcher.

In September, I developed a urinary tract infection and reacted to the medication. We had been disappointed when the pilgrimage had been cancelled, but neither of us would have been fit enough for the trip.

Our Volvo, which had been playing up off and on the whole year, worsened in November. It was costing us a small fortune just to keep it on the road.

The Omega Writers' Organisation held a conference on the Sunshine Coast. I had attended the previous year's gathering in Brisbane and learned so much about writing, we booked a room at the *Nautilus* in Mooloolaba. Colin and I had a delightful four nights going for walks in the morning before the lectures and workshops commenced. The conference helped bring my manuscripts to publication standard.

December was busy with Christmas celebrations at Colin's woodwork clubs and my writing groups. We, who always kept to ourselves, now made new friends. We went to *The Mikado* and Bizet's *Carmen*, two excellent operas. *Carmen* is a story of love, lust and jealousy. The overture swelled with excitement, and the opening scene, complete with orange trees, set the mood. Toreadors, banderilleros and flamenco dancers, added colour and charm to the scenes. The performers had been carefully selected—the American mezzo-soprano capturing the audience with her flashing eyes and passionate singing. The tenor too, was convincing, both visually and vocally. He sang with expression and his acting skills were impressive. For days after, the lively tune of the Toreador Song rang in our ears.

We celebrated Christmas at Movie World's Winter Wonderland. Like the Disneyland Christmas at Hong Kong, there was the Disney parade, lots of artificial snow and entertainment. Being young at heart, Colin and I enjoyed ourselves just as much as the children around us.

2012 had been a frustrating year with illness, our tour cancellation, and our car's frequent breakdowns. Despite all this, we knew we had been fortunate…

Chapter 21

A Rewarding Year, 2013

2013 TURNED OUT TO BE OUR busiest year. Even busier than our working days. Colin devoted his time to polishing the pieces he had skilfully crafted and learning how to make a jewellery box. 'One of my ancestors was a French polisher,' he reminded me. I noted the pride in his voice and marvelled at the fine workmanship. The box was cushioned inside and encased in leather with studs laid out in a beautiful geometrical design. I used it to store the jewellery Colin had given me over the years.

In late January 2013, Cyclone Oswald struck the east coast of North Queensland and heavy rain inundated coastal areas. Mundubbera, Eidsvold, Gayndah and Bundaberg were severely hit. My heart went out to the city of Bundaberg where I had attended several Writers' Festivals.

In February, Colin had cataract surgery. The ophthalmologist removed the opaque lens from his left eye and replaced it with a clear one. The operation proved so successful he had the other eye done a few months later. The improvement in his sight was a great help, especially when doing woodwork.

I spent much of my time attending writing workshops and author talks. More confident now, I entered writing competitions. Our interest in orchids also grew, and so did our orchid collection. Colin bought a small metal shade house, before dismantling his timber-framed one.

Barry Gable, the owner of a shade-house business, suggested, 'You should join an Orchid Society. It will help you learn more about orchids.'

'Do you have any particular one in mind?' Colin asked.

'You could join either the Eastern Districts Orchid Society in Manly West, or the Redlands Orchid Society. They're not too far from where you are.'

After the completion of our new shade house, we joined both Orchid Societies, and attended their monthly meetings. We enjoyed growing orchids and loved meeting people with the same interests. Barry Gable was the president of EDOS and a member of ROS, so we met him again there. He introduced us to his wife Ann and his sister-in-law Margaret. We also came to know other members, and found we had many interests in common, besides orchids. Our circle of friends widened.

Colin felt comfortable working with plants, so he added more orchids to his collection. At first, he grew cattleyas, then he became interested in slipper orchids. 'They are named slipper orchids because the lip of their flower forms a pouch that resembles a woman's shoe,' he explained to me.

They were expensive. I began to wonder whether this hobby was more suitable to the affluent than to average people like us.

'I only buy small plants that don't cost much,' Colin said, when I remarked at their cost.

'You've become an orchidophile.'

His reply astounded me. 'Yes. I'm afraid I have. I read about the ghost orchid the other day. It looks like a frog's ghost leaping in mid-air. It's called a *Polyrrhizza lindenii*.' Having had some uncanny experiences in his life, Colin was fascinated by ghosts.

'Are you going to buy one?'

'It'll be beyond our means. Besides, it may not be suitable to our subtropical climate. It is native to a more tropical climate like Cuba and the Everglades in Florida.'

'Many orchid growers spend thousands of dollars for a single plant,' I said. 'I've heard of some high-profile medical practitioners, who have given up their careers to grow orchids. They want to have the best, the most exotic and the rarest orchid at any cost. They must be obsessed by orchids. Hope you never do that.'

Colin grinned. 'The petals of slipper orchids look like a sexy woman's lips, and their intoxicating fragrance can cloud a person's judgement. They have sexual overtones. Did you know that the word orchid means 'testicle' in Greek?

I leaned forward and inhaled the sweet fragrance of an orchid. 'I believe they have Viagra-like powers. In Chinese medicine, they're used as an aphrodisiac. I suppose that's why orchids are so expensive.' I held up a flowering cattleya. 'Do you know that in Marcel Proust's book, *Swann's Way*, the protagonist made a pretence of re-arranging the *Cattleya* orchid in his lady's bodice so that he could touch her breast?'

'No. But I'm not surprised.'

'So now, the expression *Do a Cattleya*, has sexual overtones.' I put down the cattleya and took a step forward. 'Apart from the sexual connotations, it *is* an expensive hobby.'

'Don't worry.' Colin tousled my hair. 'We don't have the money to buy anything above two figures. All I want is to admire their beauty, inhale their perfume and enjoy growing them. Besides each other, all we need is health, happiness and a comfortable home.'

Colin had been cautious in share trading, and I was confident he would not spend our meagre savings on anything expensive. *First things first* had always been his motto.

I smiled. 'You may not realise it, but I'm getting hooked too. I love their beauty and their perfume. I am also fascinated by those with strange shapes like the Flying Duck Orchid, the Monkey Face Orchid, the Swaddled Babies, the Hooker's lips and the Naked Man Orchids.'

Monthly meetings at two orchid clubs kept us busy. Also each month, Colin took me to writers' group meetings at Palm Beach, Carindale, Victoria Point and to Milton. Yet he never showed any impatience or reluctance except to refer to himself as my *chauffeur*. He would do some shopping and try to make the most of his time while I was at meetings.

The next month found us at Reality Bites in Cooroy—a non-fiction writers' festival. I was now writing my memoirs.

'It's time for a break or we'll soon reach breaking point,' Colin said, when the festival was over. 'All work and no play…'

'…makes Jack a dull boy.' I have a terrible habit of ending his sentences, but he never showed any annoyance.

'I've checked up on a mining town—Lightning Ridge. We could go down a few mines and try our hand at fossicking.'

'That *would* be fun,' I said. 'I've never been to the outback.'

'The town has an open-air artesian pool. Just imagine soaking in a mineral bath beneath the stars.'

'How relaxing! Let's go!'

In early May, we left home at six in the morning and, as the sun climbed high in the sky, we arrived at the arid plain of Lightning Ridge. On our first day, we took a tour of the town. I marvelled at the lunar landscape of mullock heaps, where the thirsty sun sucked the earth dry.

The bus driver amused us with colourful tales of the mining town. 'Lightning Ridge is the only place in Australia, and one of the few places in the world, where black opal is found. Fossickers come here in winter and dig for opals, but they return to their homes in the summer when it gets too warm.'

I turned to Colin and squeezed his arm. 'Perhaps we'll find one before we leave.'

He patted my hand. 'That'll be the day!'

The bus stopped at a house made of glass bottles and at the Astronomer's Castle. 'We come across the most eccentric people here,' our guide said. 'This cement structure was built by a Polish miner in honour of his countryman, Copernicus, the famed mathematician and astrologer. Further on, we'll see Amigo's Castle, a creative but incomplete gothic-inspired home built by an opal miner.'

The turrets, towers and parapets of Amigo's Castle thrilled me.

We went down an opal mine with the tour group. We had been to a gold mine at Kalgoorlie, but opal mines are so different. They are usually from 6 to 18 meters beneath the surface, whereas gold mines sometimes descend two kilometres or more.

Over the next few days, we visited other mines; some deep and narrow, others rambling sideways. Our favourite was the Chamber of the Black Hand Mine. No longer a working mine, the chambers held over 500 sculptures of various subjects. The Egyptian Chamber with hieroglyphics and a replica of an Egyptian tomb made me feel I was in Egypt. A carving of the crucifixion was so life-like I involuntarily stretched out my hand to touch the blood of Christ.

Surprises awaited around every corner. A pack of gorillas peered at us, and a leprechaun grinned from a recess. A sculpture of lions slept peacefully among the rocky walls and a carving of a leaping leopard startled me. I stepped back and stumbled against Colin, who held his hand out to protect me from falling.

A black panther crouched from a cliff-edge, ready to pounce. I jumped out of its way, then embarrassed by my reaction, went back to stroke it while Colin took a photo of my daring deed.

Ned Kelly with his home-made iron mask stood near a carving of Michelangelo's David. German shepherds, spaniels, bloodhounds, and dogs of various pedigrees wagged their tails at us. The three monkeys depicting 'See no Evil. Hear no evil. Speak no Evil' each had its own niche.

We were delighted to watch the artist, Ron Conlin, at work. He stopped painting to speak to us. We could have remained there the whole day but, wanting to make the most of our visit, we re-traced our steps to enjoy the paintings and carvings once more. Finally, we visited the opal shop and returned with two opal rings and a pair of opal earrings.

We headed home after trying our luck at fossicking.

I posted a pair of opal earrings to Rose the next morning. We had been writing long emails weekly and growing closer. In September, Rose and Pat flew to South America to explore ancient ruins—the Temple of the Sun in Cusco, the ruins at Machu Picchu, Quito in Peru, the Galapagos Islands in Ecuador and the Panama Canal.

They flew back to Perth via Brisbane and stayed at the Marriot Hotel on the banks of the Brisbane River for two nights. Rose paid for one night's accommodation and valet parking for us. 'I'm sorry Rose has lavished so much money on us,' I said to Colin. 'It hurts me to see her pour out her hard-earned savings on such luxuries.'

Colin shrugged. 'You know your sister. That is the way she is. You cannot change her.'

The next morning, the four of us headed for Noosa National Park, a two-hour drive north from Brisbane. Rose and I sat in the back, and she chatted all the way. She was always the talkative one. How I prized our time together. Rose adored nature and enjoyed the walk along the trails.

On our return to Brisbane, she treated us to a sumptuous dinner in honour of their 43rd wedding anniversary. That evening, we bid her and Pat a painful farewell, wondering when we would see them again. I missed her already. *If only she did not live so far away!*

Within a couple of days after Rose's departure, we attended the Redland Library's Gala Night. My short story *Hunger* had been selected as one of the winning entries for their 2013 anthology. My friend, Margaret Dakin, won first prize.

The Mayor, Karen Williams, presented me with a trophy as well as a hundred-dollar voucher for books. My hands shook with joy as I stepped forward to receive it. That was the start of my writing journey.

Colin rejoiced with me. He had always escorted me to writers' meetings, workshops and conferences. I had gone this far because of him.

I thanked the Lord for my delightful husband and for my recent success.

November came, and so did Colin's UK cousin Terry and his wife Inga for their second visit. We picked them up from Brisbane's *Inn on the Park* and spent the whole day together as Terry planned to retire and would not be travelling so far in future.

December ended with an abundance of Christmas parties and entertainments.

Chapter 22

More Milestones, 2014

HOT AND HUMID WEATHER USHERED IN the new year, making us as languid as the drooping roses in our garden. After a week of sweltering heat, the skies opened, and refreshing rain poured down. Everything was renewed. New growth. New life. Hope!

Revitalised by the cooler conditions, Colin said, 'Our home needs a fresh coat of paint.'

'We'll give it a spring-cleaning,' I said.

Although well into summer, the freshness of the air promoted a feeling of spring. Day after day, we cleared each room, in turn, of furniture. I sorted through everything, setting aside unwanted clothes, books, furniture and utensils for the St Vincent de Paul Society. Each article of clothing held a history—a memory. As I reluctantly parted with them each book flooded my mind with the joy and satisfaction I had derived when reading it. But sorting out my collection of teddy bears was painful. I hung on to my furry treasures, yet realised the time had come to select the ones to keep. I toiled over my decision and finally gave 30 bears for Vinnies, hoping they would find a loving home. I recalled the 16 dolls I had left behind when evacuating from Rangoon to escape the invading Japanese forces in 1941, and wrenched myself from my teddy bears, keeping only a few of the most beloved and valuable ones.

Life continued happily for Queenslanders, but further south, in Victoria, temperatures reached over 40° C in the Grampians, starting fires. Halls Gap was evacuated, and relief centres for hundreds of evacuees set up in Horsham, Stawell and Ararat. Fortunately, by January 21, the fires were contained, and tourists were able to visit the Grampians National Park over the Australia Day long weekend. Halls Gap was saved once again. Through dust and heat, it had risen from disaster and defeat.

In February, I won the Narrative Hook Competition run by Omega Writers for the opening lines of my memoir. How delighted I was to reach this second milestone on my writing journey. But I was a slave to my desires and yearned for more triumphs.

Colin received several prizes for his orchids, so he commenced designing a bigger and better orchid house. Our enthusiasm was unlimited, but we realised we had stretched ourselves too far, and decided to drop at least one of our activities, so we resigned from the Catholic Historical Society as it entailed driving to the city and dining at the Irish Club after meetings.

I was reluctant to cut back on anything else and attended every meeting of my writing groups and orchid clubs.

During the year, Rose wrote of pain that ran down the side of her ribcage, of the pain killers she took, and the salt baths she was having. Rose's life superimposed itself upon mine. I could not get it out of my mind that I was so happy and well, yet my young sister lived in constant pain. I could not hear of her distress without worrying and agonising with her.

Because of her burgeoning interest in our family history, Rose wanted to know more of our past. I emailed her, describing the important events before her birth as well as those she had been too young to remember. In return, she related stories of her time in Mandalay, while I had been teaching with the nuns in missionary schools. I included these events in my memoir. Our relationship grew closer.

In May, Colin took me to the Bundaberg WriteFest at the Central Queensland University Campus. I was excited, as my friend Kathy Stewart and I had been selected for the Masterclass by Jo Butler, literary fiction editor of Harper Collins. While we attended the first day's Masterclass, Colin spent Saturday chatting with Kathy's husband Ron.

After another session with Jo Butler the next morning, we drove back to Brisbane. Bursting with enthusiasm I told Colin about the Masterclass. 'Jo spoke highly of the excerpts from my novel.'

Nothing is more contagious than enthusiasm.

By July, the new orchid house was ready. We were so proud of it because Colin had done all the work on the eight by seven by three metre shadehouse. I had helped by climbing up a tall ladder to pull the shade cloth into place.

Meanwhile, my writing career was going full steam ahead. My story, *Love at First Sight*, was shortlisted in the Lane Cove Literary Awards Competition, and my short story, *June's Death*, published in the Grieve 2014 Anthology.

I was invited to Newcastle for the Grieve Anthology Awards' Night. On the way to Newcastle, we dropped in at Tinonee Orchid Nursery to buy some exotic orchids, thus encompassing my writing career with Colin's hobby.

Newcastle was cold and windy that August. Battered by the wind, we checked in at the reception hall in the Great Western Hotel. After supper of biscuits and hot cocoa, we cuddled down for the night.

The next morning, we set out for Fort Scratchley. A howling gale buffeted us as we climbed the hill to look at the only Australian cannons ever fired upon an enemy ship. Built in 1876, with new guns installed later, the fort was constructed as a coastal defence installation to defend the city against a possible Russian attack.

Russia never attacked Newcastle, but their ship HIRMS *Rynda* entered the port in 1888 on a supposedly goodwill mission by the Grand Duke and his entourage. Newcastle officials drove them on a sight-seeing tour of the city and the fort. A local newspaper reported that coded messages were sent to St. Petersburg the next day but, fortunately, Fort Scratchley's cannons were not needed against the Russians.

However, during World War II, a Japanese submarine known as the 1-21, silently slipped into the Hunter River and shelled Newcastle. The captain in charge at Newcastle Fort, hearing the burst of shells, ordered his gun crew to return fire. The guns of Fort Scratchley blazed at the submarine. It dived and fled for safety but prowled the sea and wreaked havoc among Allied shipping for the next five months until November 1943, when it was depth charged by US vessels. None of the crew survived.

Colin and I were interested in history, and I was particularly eager to learn more about the invasion of Burma by Japanese troops.

We took a siesta after our visit to Fort Scratchley and, that evening, I wore my red and black evening dress for the presentation of prizes at the Newcastle Conservation Centre. We were ushered to our seats and a choir entertained us while we waited for the winners to be announced. When my name was called, I went up with shaking limbs to receive my prize. My dream had been a seedling that now turned into a sapling.

Earlier in the year, I had entered the first three chapters of my yet-unpublished memoir to the Barnados Great Aussie Book Competition and been awaiting the results. Not long after our return from Newcastle, I was requested to send in my full manuscript for perusal, because my memoir had been selected as one of the finalists. I waited, breathless, for the results.

Three weeks' later, a spokeswoman from Barnados emailed to inform me that my story had failed to win the competition because it was not set in Australia. I did not know whether to be happy or sad. I was elated my work was considered as a finalist for the award yet saddened because it was not a winner. All the same, 2014 had been a great boon to my writing career, and the flower of gratitude blossomed in my soul.

We were celebrating Christmas with dinner at our orchid club, when news of the siege at Lindt Café in Sydney reached us. Acts of terrorism we had so often seen on television struck us with fear. Fear turned to terror and heightened in intensity when television and social media gave real-time coverage as the tragedy unfolded. We were rivetted to the screen, watching and praying for the eighteen hostages held by the Iranian-born terrorist, Man Haron Monis.

During the rescue, when police forced their way in, the terrorist brutally shot the café manager, Tori Johnson, before he was gunned down by the liberators. Unfortunately, a stray bullet killed one of the hostages.

Shaken by the unfolding of events, I reflected on the fragility of life. For days after, the joy in my achievements was subdued as I meditated on the suddenness of death. I felt vulnerable and sought safety in prayer. Bertie was the only member of my family whose death had not come unexpectedly. My mother died without any warning, and meningitis carried off my baby brother Trevor within 24 hours. My eldest brother Rupert's death from tetanus had been sudden and unexpected. My beloved sister June was struck by plague in Mandalay during World War II. All my siblings except Bertie had been incredibly young when God called them to Him. One by one, I had seen them depart. *What will it be like when God calls me? Will it be at night, like Mum or during the day like the others?* Only the Lord can tell. But death is the ultimate deadline and I never like to be rushed.

Ten days later, as the title of Shakespeare's play, *All's Well that Ends Well* reminded us, we spent Christmas 2014 at O'Reilly's Rain Forest Retreat in Lamington National Park, on the Green Mountains, reflecting on the year's achievements.

Chapter 23

Trials & Triumphs, 2015

On 19 January 2015, our first mishap of the year occurred after an Orchid Society meeting. On our way home, a storm erupted, thunder rolled, lightning flashed, and sheets of rain obscured our vision. Unable to proceed, we pulled off the road and waited until the storm abated. The roadsides were running rivers, the road slippery and even with the car lights on high beam, visibility was only a few feet ahead.

'Will the roads be flooded and cut us off?' I asked Colin.

'There'll be some local flooding but hopefully, we'll be able to get through.' His eyes were on the road.

'Don't take any risks.'

Cars sped past, throwing up water and impeding our vision. I gripped the sides of my seat and braced myself for an accident, but our new tyres held their ground.

We reached home late that evening, only to find our garden turned into a lake. My pulse raced. *Was our home flooded?* We parked the car outside the garage and waded towards the entrance of our house. If the water rose another couple of millimetres, part of our home would be submerged.

Colin set off to find the cause and returned after a few minutes with a shovel in his hand. 'Our retaining wall has collapsed and is blocking the drainage system.'

He waved me back when I went to help him. 'Stay out of the rain. I don't want you getting sick. I can manage on my own.' He shovelled away all the dirt and debris blocking the path to the storm-water drains.

Inch by inch, the water receded.

Three weeks later, in February 2015, Cyclone Marcia struck Shoalwater Bay and caused major damage to several houses at Yeppoon, Rockhampton and along the Capricorn Coast. How true is the saying, 'It never rains but it pours.' In the past months, everyone had prayed for rain because of the drought. Yet when it did come, it caused mayhem.

We were grateful Redlands only received the edge of the weather, but it inspired Colin to ensure our property was safe from flooding. He spent the next few days building a higher and stronger retaining wall to divert the water to the storm-water drains. Then he turned his attention to our roses. The drought had killed most of them. Out of 72 bushes only 24 had survived, so he converted four rose beds back into lawn and transplanted the remaining bushes into two beds.

'Roses are an expensive hobby,' Colin said. 'Perhaps we shouldn't have grown them. First, we were troubled by aphids, then it was black spot. Now this…' Broken branches lay scattered all over our garden. Our biggest and best custard apple tree had keeled over—roots and all.

Our losses, although worrisome for us, were small in comparison to others. Cyclone Marcia had left a trail of destruction along its path with extensive damage to townships. Roofs were ripped off and trees uprooted.

Colin cut the fallen tree into manageable lengths and took them to the tip. Finally, chainsaw in hand, he climbed a ladder and set to work on the pecan tree where dismembered branches hung precariously. One by one, they fell to the ground while I stood at a safe distance below and waited to drag them away.

His grip must have slackened, because the chainsaw slipped, and dropped from his hand. I rushed forward to turn it off while he climbed down, blood streaming from his left hand. My heart stopped. I grew cold. I visualised a handless arm. We washed the blood off, but it kept flowing, soaking the wad of cotton I held to stem the flow of gore.

I panicked at the sight of so much blood. 'You need to see a surgeon, and have it stitched.'

'No. I'll put some paw paw ointment on. It'll soon heal.'

'Should I call an ambulance?'

Colin pushed me aside. 'There's work to be done!'

Fortunately, the saw had dropped from Colin's hand before it had worked its way through tendon, nerves and bone. But it left its imprints on his hand, like a pair of pinking shears does to a piece of material. I shivered at the sight of the jagged marks.

Colin put on the ointment, and I bandaged his hand. The wound kept bleeding for a long time, and remained sore for weeks but eventually healed.

Colin could not keep away from his favourite pastime, bushwalking. On March 1, after repairing most of the storm damage, we drove to Lamington National Park. The bush tracks were wet and slippery. Fallen trees obstructed our path; we went around or over them. During the storm, orchids dislodged from the higher branches, lay on the track, helpless and begging for a home. Rather than let them die, we picked them up and placed them in the forked branches of trees, where they would survive and bring joy to others.

The fresh and cool air filled us with delight. How lovely it all was, especially after those hot humid days earlier in the year.

One morning in April, my face turned red, and a rash appeared on my neck. Colin googled 'rashes' and found some facial creams. He put in an order and they arrived from the US in time for my birthday. The rash on my face left but reappeared on other parts of my body. I took baths in potassium permanganate and in magnesium sulphate and used nourishing creams. The rash came and went. On my legs. On my arms. On my torso.

My GP, who specialised in skin problems, took blood tests, and gave me a biopsy. 'Tests show that you have dermatitis,' he said. 'Synthetic clothing irritates your skin. Avoid any contact with them.'

I went on a cotton-buying spree. Cotton underwear. Cotton tops and cotton shorts and slacks. I took all my synthetic clothes to Vinnies but, despite all my efforts, the dermatitis simply shifted from one place to another.

Meanwhile, Colin's interest in orchids was growing. He took out 1st, 2nd and 3rd prizes in the novice hybrid section and received a trophy as Novice Champion of the Year in the Redlands Orchid Show. We both enjoyed growing orchids, but Colin did all the work, fertilising, watering and re-potting them when required.

Gavin, a member of our orchid club, donated his deceased wife's orchids to fellow members. We gratefully received some twenty orchids to re-pot. Gavin also gave two shade houses to the club. Names of interested members were put into a hat and two lucky winners drawn. We won the bigger shade house, but I knew Colin would not be able to dismantle and load it on our trailer without help. His hand was still sore from his encounter with the chainsaw. *What should I do?*

Daphne, the winner of the 2nd prize, stormed up to me. 'I want the *large* shade house.'

At first, I was annoyed by her aggressive tone, but soon a flood of joy washed away my irritability. My prayer was answered. 'I'll swap this for the small one.'

We smiled and commenced to dismantle our prizes.

With his sore hand, Colin undid the bolts and nuts of the shade house, while I helped hold up the walls in the hot sun. Daphne and Kevin lent us their tools to undo the staples from the shade cloth and borrowed our pliers.

My face grew hotter and redder and itchier but, before dark, we managed to dismantle the shade house and cart it home. We could not have done that with the bigger prize. From then on, Daphne and I became the best of friends and would always sit together at the Redland orchid growers' meetings.

Colin's orchid collection grew steadily, and we needed more space. By June, he commenced reassembling the framework of his shade house in a suitable spot. I helped by holding up the sides while he stapled the shade cloth on the framework. Within a week, we had a new orchid house.

In early September, I met a Christian publisher who was interested in my book *Chocolate Soldier: The Story of a Conchie*. By the end of the month, I signed a contract with another publisher, Armour Books, for my memoir, *Heaven Tempers the Wind: Story of a War Child*.

O joy of joys! God was granting me all my dreams.

Before the month was over, I was shortlisted in the Toowoomba Writers' Fest Literary Competition, and my short story, *The Derelict*, was published in their 2015 Anthology.

I was invited to the presentations. My cup of joy spilled over.

Meanwhile, my skin condition escalated. My legs itched so much I scratched in my sleep. They bled. I asked my GP for a referral to a dermatologist, who prescribed prednisone tablets and a cortisone ointment. He told me that food had nothing to do with my condition, so I sought comfort in eating. I knew I was allergic to milk, but I loved chocolate. We visited the chocolate factory in Maleny, and Colin bought me lots of dark chocolate. The rash disappeared for a time but reappeared like a naughty sprite after a few weeks. I continued writing and tried my best to ignore the itch. It proved to be an impossible task. Little did I realise my rash was growing worse because I had indulged in my favourite foods, not knowing I was allergic to them. My stress levels heightened, the rash grew red and furious, and my hair began to fall out when trying to keep up with the publisher's deadlines.

Rose suggested going to hospital if I also had pain. Fortunately, there was no pain. Only an intense itch that maddened me, and bouts of scratching and bleeding.

As I was getting bald, Colin bought me a beret. Friends wished me *Bonjour*. I attempted a smile.

Rose and I continued emailing. Once, when reminiscing about the past, she told me she had missed me when I first left home to teach in a mission school in Northern Burma. I was surprised because she had not shown any sorrow at my departure. I wish I had known it then, because it would have endeared her to me even more.

On the other hand, Winston had said, 'If you love me, why do you leave me?'

My heart bled to hear his words, but I had been thinking of joining the Columban nuns at the time and needed to answer God's call. The Columbans were missionary sisters founded in Ireland in 1922, who had been stationed in Myitkyina. Touched by their spirit of joy and charity, I had hoped to enter their novitiate in Ireland.

In early October, Rose and her daughter Eileen flew out to Jordan as they were keen to visit the ancient city of Petra. They also visited the Dead Sea, and Rose brought me back a mud mask that helped soothe my skin.

Frustrated with the length of time my skin was taking to heal, Colin took me to an allergy specialist. After a Scratch Test the specialist put me on a diet and recommended non-addictive antihistamines that were less harmful than the prednisone tablets prescribed by the dermatologist.

I was allergic to latex, besides other things. We had been using a latex mattress for some years, so Colin bought a latex-free one. I took particular care of my diet and only ate non-allergenic food. My skin slowly began to improve.

St Augustine's words, 'Troubles are but so many instructors to teach men wit,' would prove to be true by the end of the following year.

Chapter 24

Surprises, 2016

My New Year's gift was a contract from Rhiza Press for my debut historical novel, *Chocolate Soldier: The Story of a Conchie*, an account of Colin's uncle during World War II. What a delightful start for the year. I knew I would be busy with all the work involved before publication, but I did not dream the year would also bring so many surprises.

In early January, my sister wrote, 'Pat and I will be going to China, Mongolia and Russia on the Trans-Siberian train in the middle of the year. Eileen is working on it, sis.'

They had been on a tour of Iceland and Eastern Europe last June, and my sister still suffered from aches and pains. On top of that, her two daughters Maureen and Eileen, had given them tickets for a cruise as a Christmas gift. I was surprised to hear she planned so many trips in one year.

In mid-February, Rose and Pat flew to Sydney and commenced their cruise on the M/S *Voyager*. My niece Maureen emailed us, saying, 'Dad has sent a message informing me they will be docking at the port of Brisbane on February 25 at 10 am.'

We were astounded, as Brisbane was not a scheduled stopover. Apparently a cyclone compelled the ship to alter course and seek shelter. I hugged Colin. Despite our differences and foibles, I loved Rose and looked forward to seeing her.

Opera, Orchids and Oz

We met them at the Treasury Casino in Brisbane. Rose looked pale and could scarcely keep her eyes open. 'I'm exhausted. I was seasick for the first four or five days.'

We brought them home and they took a shower. While Colin and Pat chatted over morning tea, I gave Rose a massage. She fell asleep on the carpet in our lounge, looking so ill and helpless, I was reminded of the time she had smallpox as an infant, and an incendiary bomb had fallen on our house during an air raid.

I covered her with a sheet and crept away to join Colin and Pat who were chatting over a cup of coffee. Pat showed us his scars from his cancer operation. 'My arm is still sore from the operation on my neck. It hurts whenever I move my arm.'

After a while, my sister awoke somewhat refreshed, and delved into her backpack. As usual, she had not come empty-handed. She gave me a beautiful black handbag and handed Colin a watch she had bought from the cruise ship. Rose showed her love through her gifts.

When the time to return to the ship drew closer, we drove them back to the city and dropped them a bus stop. A lump rose to my throat as the bus drove off towards the ship terminal and Rose waved with that sad look like Mum's. I thanked the Lord for sending my sister to me.

Maureen was a lawyer and extremely interested in family history. She and her husband Travis had just returned from a holiday in Burma, and she was so excited about visiting Rose's birthplace, she asked us whether we would like to tour the country with her parents. When we replied in the affirmative, she drew up an itinerary for us.

Her plans fell through when Rose showed no interest in them. I was disappointed, as I would have loved to see the old, familiar places with my sister and show Colin the house we had lived in after the war.

In March, I caught my foot in a wire, tripped, and fell heavily on the concrete verandah of the Holland Park library. Scans revealed a full thickness tear of the biceps-tendon, supraspinatus, and the infraspinatus, as well as a partial thickness tear in the sub acromial/ sub deltoid bursa. In short, half my tendons of the right shoulder were torn, and the right knee was bruised and sore. I seemed to be getting accident-prone.

Then our orchids looked sick. 'It looks like they have been hit by a virus,' a friend said. 'Dump them in the tip.'

Our hearts ached as we sorted out 42 plants. So much love and hard work had gone into caring for them. But to prevent the virus from spreading and have the whole lot wiped out, we took the ailing orchids to the tip.

Rose wrote to offer her sympathies to me regarding my accident and to Colin for the loss of our orchids. Our troubles brought us closer. She poured out her sorrows to me. 'I'm dying inside, and I cannot do anything about it.' She had been worrying over Winston, who lived like a recluse and never went to a doctor.

I empathised with her, but said nothing, recalling the time she said, 'If I want your advice, I'll ask you for it.' It had angered me, and I did not want to go through that again.

In April, Rose sent us a card for ANZAC Day—the day of her arrival in Australia from the UK. Grateful to us for having sponsored her passage, she invariably sent *Thank You* cards at ANZAC. Her profuse thanks embarrassed me as I had only done what Mum had requested.

Winston must have had a change of heart, because he considered selling his house and moving in with Rose. He told me he was giving his piano to her in gratitude for putting him up in her home when they had arrived from the UK. Gratitude is the foundation of happiness, and I hoped his soul would blossom.

In her emails, Rose continued to reminisce about all the old times in Burma as well as her wedding with Pat. On her return from the holiday on the Siberian Express, she sent me a souvenir magnet and said that Maureen would bring me a gift when she came to Brisbane. Knowing my weakness for dolls, Rose had sent me a Babushka on a previous holiday.

A few weeks later, Maureen emailed, saying that her employers, Shine Lawyers, would be holding a seminar, followed by a dinner-dance in Brisbane's City Hall on August 5.

It was lovely to see my niece, whom we did not really know well. She was a charming girl—pretty and poised.

That month, my friend, Mother Irene from Burma, sent me the sad news of the death of my old friend Mother Rose. The two of us had entered the novitiate at Toungoo together, where we had trained for three years until her transfer to Kalaw, a missionary convent on the Shan Plateau. She had taken her final vows after another three years, but I left the convent.

Soon after Mother Irene's letter, Mother Josephine, another former companion, invited me to Burma for her diamond jubilee, but we were unable to go at such short notice. Besides, I was preparing for the book launch of my memoir, *Heaven Tempers the Wind: Story of a War Child*.

The book launch in September was memorable. I am so grateful to the staff of Victoria Point Library for this favour. My publisher, Anne Hamilton, introduced me to the audience and I gave a short talk, which was followed by refreshments. Three friends from the Carindale Writers' Group, Debbie Raymond, Leslee-Anne Hewson and Dorothy Vicary, as well as Laurie, Marci and Sara from the Victoria Point Writers' Group, came to give their support and buy my book. Jill Smith from the Gold Coast Writers' Group was also present. It was a long way to come, and I was grateful to my friends for their ongoing encouragement.

By the end of September, another surprise awaited us. An email came from Dr James Cooper of Tabor College, South Australia: 'It gives me great pleasure to confirm that your story, *The Three Miracles*, has been accepted for publication in the forthcoming Stories of Life Anthology.'

He ended by thanking me for 'my beautifully written and thought-provoking contribution.'

The story was about Rose's miraculous recovery from smallpox during the war. How well I recall that day. Never did I realise that, by the grace of God, I would one day write about this momentous event in our lives. Never did I realise too, that it would bring me closer to achieving my dream of being an author.

The following month, Rose and Eileen went on a holiday to Mexico and Cuba. On their return, my sister emailed that she would be sending us souvenirs via Maureen, who would be coming to Brisbane again in November. Delighted, we looked forward to my niece's visit.

Maureen came and left like a whirlwind. Unlike her visit in August, her plane arrived during a storm and was kept in a holding position before being allowed to land. Colin and I huddled in the parking bay at the airport, trying to shelter from heavy winds that damaged a Qantas plane at the airport and smashed containers awaiting shipment.

Debris landed in the Brisbane River, damaging vessels, so we were fortunate not to receive any injury.

Maureen arrived, fresh and elegant with her charming smile and delightful manners. To our joy, she spent one night with us before leaving for a conference in Toowoomba. We grew to love her during those two visits in August and November.

2016 had been an extremely busy year but a lucky one too. My skin was now smooth as a baby's bottom with no signs of rash. My family ties had grown stronger and our love for orchids was bringing Colin and I even closer than ever before. *Deo gratias!*

Chapter 25

Falls, Family, Friends & Feasting, 2017

ON TUESDAY 28 MARCH 2017, Cyclone Debby hit Airlie Beach and unleashed her fury all the way from the Whitsunday Region of Central Queensland right through to Lismore in north-eastern New South Wales. Major flooding and damage to houses and crops occurred with some 20,000 people were evacuated.

Cyclone Debby also left its mark upon me. It brought heavy winds to Brisbane and the mat on the back verandah—an off-cut of our carpet—curled up with a snarl. On April Fools' Day, after lunch, while taking some leftovers to the bin, I tripped on the mat and hit my head on the concrete floor. I tried to get up but could not. Hanging on to a nearby chair, I dragged myself to my knees and shouted for help.

Colin was at my side in seconds. 'Are you all right? What happened?'

No sooner was I upright than a dark cloud swept over my eyes, and my knees gave way. I collapsed in a heap. Colin must have helped break my fall, but all I can recall is finding myself on my back, with him bending over me. 'You fainted. You must have fractured something. I can't lift you. I've sent for an ambulance.'

Like a parrot, I repeated his words. 'Fractured? Ambulance?' I tried to get up, but pain shot through my body.

'Just be still,' Colin said, pressing me gently down.

The ambulance arrived within a short time. 'Would you like a pain killer?' the paramedic asked.

'No thank you. I want to be fully aware of what happens to me.' I remembered the shot of penicillin that had put me into a semi-conscious state during my pregnancy.

The ambulance carried me off to Redland Hospital, where we were forced to wait in a queue for hours. I lay there wondering what was causing the delay. Eventually, the senior paramedic informed me the staff had told them to take me to the Princess Alexander Hospital.

'Why?' I asked.

'Because you could be suffering from concussion, and they have no facilities in case you need an operation.'

All this without even seeing me first!

I was carted off and admitted to the Princess Alexandra Hospital. After another long delay, my lower back was x-rayed. I had fractured my pelvis in several places.

This appalling lack of hospital facilities in Queensland made me wonder how Australia would cope if war ever reached our shores. I recalled the time in Burma when, after the bombing by Japanese planes in 1941, wounded were left in hospital corridors, awaiting treatment while they bled to death.

My sister Rose was full of advice and sympathy. She phoned Colin several times and also rang the hospital to inquire after me. Unfortunately, I was unable to reach the phone and could not take any calls. I knew she was concerned about my fall. Frustrated, I lay there, feeling forgotten by the staff on duty. At the time, I did not possess a mobile phone, and only then did I bemoan my lack.

On one occasion, a nurse happened to be passing and I called out to her. She stopped, and hearing the ringing tones of my phone, handed it to me. I took it gratefully and explained to Rose why I could not answer her calls previously.

Hospital stays are not pleasant and my two weeks at the PA were even worse than I expected. The hospital was understaffed, and the nurses overworked. I wondered whether life would ever be normal again. *Will I be able to walk again? Will I be bed-ridden for the rest of my life? Is this the beginning of the end?* I requested a transfer to Greenslopes and, after several delays, was finally moved to their rehabilitation unit.

Colin visited me daily. One evening, he brought a beautiful bouquet of flowers signed by the residents of our street. 'Maggie saw the paramedics driving off with you in the ambulance. She looked shocked, and asked me what had happened.'

I was so touched by the lovely blooms and the kindness of all those who had signed the Get-Well card. The residents were friendly, but I only had a nodding acquaintance with most of them. Maggie's husband, Mike, would wave to us whenever he walked down to catch the bus to work. Others would wave from their cars if we were in the garden when they drove past. Connie and James, who lived opposite, always left a Christmas Card in our letterbox at Christmas time. The neighbours were young. Some of their children attended private colleges, others state schools. However, they all had grown up on the same street and played together. They celebrated birthdays, Christmas and Australia Day together. Now they sent flowers. Friends from my writing groups and orchid clubs brought flowers and gifts. I never realised anyone knew or cared about me because we had always kept to ourselves.

At Greenslopes, I shared a private ward with a diabetic patient, who had colitis. Each morning, she would awake early, and moan with pain. That would wake me until a nurse hurried in and gave her medication. Then we both would fall into a fitful sleep.

One night, a nurse awakened me. 'Wake up. It's time for your shot of insulin.'

It took some time to convince her that my *neighbour* needed the needle, not *me*.

The next night, the same nurse awoke me. 'It's time to change your nappy.'

Half asleep, I raised myself on my elbow and snapped. 'I *don't* use nappies.'

Once again, the nurse realised her error and left. Fully awake, I lay there and longed for Colin. For home. For normal meals. At the same time, I realised how lucky I was to have survived the fall.

Despite the disturbed nights, I attended rehabilitation sessions twice daily. I met other patients and, on hearing their harrowing tales, was thankful for not needing an operation like so many of them. Every day, exhausted and hungry after my workouts in the gym, I had biscuits for morning and afternoon tea. Because of my allergy to milk, I soon had asthma attacks from the ingredients in the biscuits. I coughed and coughed. This set me back and I had to resort to a Ventolin inhaler. My appetite diminished and I lost weight.

After being in hospital for three weeks, despite my setbacks, I asked for and received weekend leave on Saturday 22 April. An intense joy overcame me as Colin drove me home, and I wandered around the house, breathing in the fresh atmosphere, and enjoying my time with him. I caught up with my emails and sent off my entry for the CALEB Competition as well as my finished manuscript to my publisher. Satisfied, I joined Colin in the garden with my wheeler. I could not enter the orchid house, but the perfume of the orchids wafted out to me as I listened to the sweet singing of Cyclops and the other butcher birds. I named my favourite Cyclops, because it had lost an eye as a fledgling, and always flew down to eat out of my hand.

After the publication of *Chocolate Soldier* and *Heaven Tempers the Wind,* I arranged with Koorong Books of Toowoomba for a book signing at their bookstore. Colin picked me up from hospital on Friday of the Labour Day weekend, which coincided with my birthday. What a delightful birthday present to spend the evening with my darling husband!

The next morning, we rose early and drove to Toowoomba after breakfast. The book signing proved a success. I sat at a table and occasionally moved around with my walker. How delighted I was to be well enough to keep my appointment with the bookstore. The people were friendly, and I sold a few books.

I graduated from a walker to a walking stick and checked out from Greenslopes on May 5. I continued my rehab exercises at the Redlands Rehabilitation Centre and did the prescribed exercises at home, intent on regaining full mobility. My muscles, which had deteriorated after my fracture, slowly regained tone and strength, but my breathing problem hung on for months.

Two days after checking out from hospital was Colin's birthday, so we drove to the Spit on the Gold Coast. I lay on a blanket beneath a tree in the dappled shade and listened to the waves crashing on the shore. The fresh sea air did me good. Slowly my health returned.

The following week, I gave a Living Books Presentation of my memoir, *Heaven Tempers the Wind* at Broadbeach Library. At first, I trembled at the thought of speaking before strangers. *Will the audience ask me embarrassing questions? Will I stammer and stutter from bashfulness?*

On the day of my presentation, I gazed at my audience, swallowed hard, and licked my dry lips. I read excerpts from my book and spoke for a few minutes, then waited for the dreaded questions…

I need not have feared. The audience were captivated by my story and questions were many and varied. Warmth rose to my cheeks as I answered them truthfully and spontaneously.

In July, when my fracture had partially healed, Colin drove me to Maleny for a book signing at Rosetta Books.

Exhausted after a busy morning, we drove home to enjoy a well-earned rest.

A few weeks' later, I gave talks at the Broadbeach and the Carindale Libraries on my debut novel, *Chocolate Soldier: The Story of a Conchie*. By now, I had lost most of my nervousness and was gaining confidence. Had I foreseen my pelvic fracture, I doubt whether I would have made any speaking engagements. However, it turned out for the best, and everything went so well, without impeding my recovery.

Not long after, I signed a contract with my publisher, Armour Books, for Part 2 of my memoirs, *The Sides of Heaven*.

A few months later, my short story, *Three Miracles*, was published in the *Gecko Renewal and Other Short Stories of Life*, by Morning Star Publication, 2017. To crown it all, I was one of the three finalists in the Australia and New Zealand-wide CALEB Competition for my memoir, *Heaven Tempers the Wind*.

Enchanted by my success, I trod on air and thanked the Lord for blessing my work and giving me the opportunity to publicise my books. I recalled the time when, I had read Louisa Alcott's *Little Women* as a child, I admired Jo March and wanted to write a book about my family like Jo. Now God had granted my wish.

I sent copies of my latest book, *The Sides of Heaven*, to Rose and Winston. Neighbours invited us to join in their Christmas celebrations. Orchid Clubs held festive dinners where Colin and I feasted and made merry. Connie, a nurse who lived opposite us, dropped in to advise me about the services available to me as an aged pensioner.

My accident had brought us closer to our neighbours and friends, and for the first time, I experienced the Australian spirit of mateship, especially in times of trial, when communities are brought together.

Christmas day found us at Green Mountains. We went to the little village church for Mass and praised the Lord for all the blessings we had received during the year. I looked forward to 2018 for a less stressful year and prayed for a return to health and fitness and for a successful writing journey.

Chapter 26

2018

IF 2017 HAD BEEN A BUSY YEAR, then 2018 was even busier. Before two months of the new year had passed, the second volume of my memoirs, *The Sides of Heaven,* was launched at the Victoria Point Library. Friends turned up, and my neighbours came as a group. The audience rained questions on me. At the end, to my immense surprise, our neighbour Maggie Baker presented me with a bouquet on behalf of friends from our street.

It was the culmination of my joy. I was so grateful to all my friends, well-wishers and the librarians who organised the book launch. Joy is the simplest form of gratitude and time stood still for me because all my dreams had been surpassed.

The library had advertised the event in our local newspaper. It brought in many other booklovers. Among them was the president of the Moreton Bay View Club, who invited me to speak at their International Women's Day luncheon. A couple of weeks' later, after a delicious lunch at the View Club, I presented my talk and sold many books as a finale.

That week, I gave a talk at the Omega Book Fair. Then in July, I was invited to speak on Burma to WeR1, a multicultural group. I grabbed the opportunity of reading some excerpts from my book about Burma, *Heaven Tempers the Wind: Story of a War Child.* Members enthused over learning a bit more of Burma, and especially the various hill tribes who, even now, are still fighting for their independence. At the conclusion of my talk, the club presented me with a bottle of excellent vintage wine.

In August, I read an excerpt from my book at an Author Showcase held in the Logan Arts Centre and the following month, I was invited to an Author Expo at Capalaba Library.

In November, on Remembrance Day, I spoke at Logan North Library. What a thrill I experienced when members of the local Returned Soldiers' League turned up at my talk and bombarded me with questions about the war in Burma, all of which I could answer because of my intense research. It gave me immense satisfaction to answer the questions of men who had fought and witnessed all the horrors and barbarity of war. Of men who had bled in various theatres of war like Korea, Vietnam, and the Middle East.

This would not have been possible without my husband's help. Colin drove me to writing events. Colin welcomed the audience. Colin took photos during my talks. Colin sold my books at the end of sessions. Throughout my stay in hospital and rehabilitation, he had exuded the patience of Job, and I owed my success to him.

Of course, it was the Lord above all else who guided my footsteps. It was God who inspired my writing and gave me so many opportunities to promote and sell my books.

Colin devoted all his private time to tending his orchid collection. He displayed them at Orchid Shows and, although a beginner, he won first, second and third prizes in the Cattleya Class at the Brisbane Orchid Show of April 2018 and received a hundred-dollar voucher as best novice of the year by the Australian Paphiopedilum Society. His orchid also carried off the Species Champion prize at the Redland Orchid Show.

I was immensely proud of my Colin, who shared his knowledge with other beginners by giving a talk on orchids at a meeting of

WeR1 in August. He also spoke to novice orchid growers at the Eastern District Orchid Society.

As time passed, the number of our shade houses increased. Orchid growing knitted us together like a plain and purl pattern. We attended meetings together, and I did my bit, helping carry the smaller and lighter orchids to meetings. It entailed long drives and late nights, but we loved each other's company, and we adored orchids.

In July, we decided to enrol in the orchid Judges' Course. The theory classes would last 18 months and the practical sessions, another three years. The study did not deter us, but we did not look forward to more late nights at orchid shows when we would be Associate Judges.

That spring, my allergy to pollens brought on respiratory problems and breathing difficulties. My condition worsened during the fires in north Queensland and Stradbroke Island. I coughed and struggled for breath, so Colin took me to a Respiratory Specialist who sent me for a lung assessment. The pulmonary specialist confirmed I had asthma with only 40% lung capacity.

I had relied on antihistamines and inhalers whenever my asthma attacks and coughing spells grew worse. The specialist prescribed steroids that had harmful side-effects and were not recommended for those suffering from cataracts or glaucoma. As I had both conditions, I feared the damage it could have on my kidneys and stopped taking the steroids after a few months.

Not long after, I found that walking downhill or descending stairs triggered off pain in my knee joints. An x-ray of my knees showed that cartilage had worn away. I guessed it was due to all the kneeling during my years in the convent.

Despite my lack of cartilage and its cushioning effect on my knees, Colin and I continued our bushwalks, but we avoided steep hills or steps. That did not leave us much choice as most national parks were hilly. I was sorry to be a drag on Colin. I knew he loved long walks above anything else, so I tried my best to exercise and keep fit. I had read that good food, exercise and contentment were great aids to success. Physical exercise became a passion.

I phoned Winston for his birthday. He didn't reply, but the following day when I rang, he said, 'When NBN comes to my place, I won't have a phone anymore, but I'll write.'

Although saddened by his words, I tried to be cheerful. 'Then even if I can't hear your voice, I'll get your letters.'

I kept phoning Winston until his phone was cut off. When I wrote, he did not reply. I concluded that his depression must be getting worse. Sadness is like a head cold, but depression is like a cancer. *Hope I will get to see him when I go to Perth,* I thought. But hope is a dream unless anchored in Christ.

Maureen invited us to stay at her home when we visited Perth in September. Thrilled, we accepted her offer, as we had grown very fond of our niece ever since she visited us the previous year.

Rose invited us to her get-together luncheon on Fathers' Day, the day of our arrival.

Eileen also emailed, inviting us for breakfast at Elizabeth Quay. My joy filled me with sunshine, and I looked forward to Perth—my final trip to WA. Colin, eager to add to his orchid collection, wanted to buy some rare specimens from a nursery over there.

Maureen and Travis met us at the airport and drove to the restaurant for the Fathers' Day celebration. I considered it the Last Supper, as I was advancing in years, and doubted whether I would get to Perth again.

We spent three delightful days with Maureen while Travis was at work. She drove us around, pointing out her favourite shops. We took advantage of the sunny days and delighted in joining her when walking Missy and Freddy in the nearby park.

On the day before their departure, we visited Thelma, an old friend of mine, and left Maureen to pack for their tour of Eastern Europe. Later, we went on to Easy Orchids, the nursery Colin had planned to visit.

The day of Maureen's and Travis's departure came all too soon. A wave of sorrow swept over us, as our love for them had increased during those few days.

Travis had lent us his car during their absence, so we met Rose and Pat at their place the next day. Pat drove us and Shiloh to King's Park. Shiloh was a sturdy boxer who whipped us painfully with her tail. However, she was as gentle as she was strong and won our affection before the day's end. We strolled along amid the wildflowers, mingling with tourists who had come from all over the world to witness the beautiful display of blooms. We enjoyed the riot of colours from Pink Everlastings, Qualup Bells, black, red, yellow and green kangaroo paws, and delighted to see the Donkey orchids, and pink Fairy orchids.

Colin and Pat walked ahead taking photos, while Rose and I followed, admiring the flowers and making the most of our time together.

We reserved the next day for a visit to Winston who lived in obscurity at his home in Fremantle. He saw no visitors, apart from his youngest daughter Sheree, but I hoped he would see me, as he had done during our trip to Perth in 2007. I pictured our meeting—the pouring out of words, the hugs and tears. But imagination is a tarnished mirror…

Wildflowers adorned either side of the road to Fremantle. We stopped to take photos and enjoy the brilliant colours. I could hardly wait to see my brother after eleven long years. Our family was dwindling with only three of us left, and I was eager to see him before either of us died.

On our arrival, I raced up the stairs of Winston's house. I had bought Winston a CD set of Cliff Richards' complete works because the singer had been one of his favourites. We pressed the doorbell and called out. No answer. We knocked and knocked at each window in case he was still asleep. Dead silence greeted us.

Choking with emotion, I left the CD with a short note on the verandah before leaving for Fremantle Harbour. The strong winds buffeted us as we made our way to a restaurant for a lunch of fish and chips. The skies turned grey, and I coughed until I gasped for breath. Cold winds never failed to bring on an asthma attack.

We returned to Winston's house after our meal, hoping and praying he would be home and let us in. The CD set and my note were no longer there. My heart leapt and lodged itself in my throat. I pressed the doorbell. *Perhaps he'll see us now*. No sound of footsteps. Nothing but the echoes of the doorbell followed by a wall of silence. I went to each window again, crying out my brother's name in despair. No greeting answered our calls.

What have I done to deserve this? I forced back my tears. I would not spoil our holiday. My Colin's holiday.

I asked Colin to take photos of me standing on the verandah where the three of us had stood so many years ago and chatted. We left after shouting out our love and our goodbyes to Winston. I recalled the disappointment I had felt when Mum died only a few months before our planned reunion with the whole family. I should have learned that disappointments cannot be avoided. Life will have them, but they are holes of sorrow that seal up with the passing of time; not vacuums that suck all joy from our lives. But at the time, I only saw the tomb of my buried hopes of a final goodbye.

The next morning, being Saturday, we visited Winston's daughter Sheree and her son Jack. It was a delightful opportunity to see our niece and god-daughter Sheree and Winston's grandson, Jack—a cute ten-year-old.

On Sunday, Rose's younger daughter Eileen, treated us to breakfast in the Brewery House at Elizabeth Quay. Eileen, also, was our goddaughter. She had been quiet and shy when holidaying with us as a teenager in Queensland. An adult now, she shed her bashfulness and was charming and sociable. Eileen worked in the Public Service and spent most of her free time helping others, indulging in a fitness programme, and running in marathon races. She had just been for a run and her husband Lance was with her.

That evening brought us together again. Eileen drove us to the recently constructed Matagarup Bridge that linked East Perth to Burswood Peninsula and the Optus Stadium. After a walk over the bridge, we took a circuit around the stadium. Eileen once again stood us a delicious meal, then took us to her home, which we had never seen. We had been to her wedding, nine years ago, but her house had yet to be built.

The home was huge. Lance had his own office and computer room. Eileen had converted another room into a gym as she was an exercise fanatic and ran in marathons and triathlons. After many hugs and kisses, we departed, wondering whether we would ever meet again.

We spent our last two days in Perth with Rose. On Monday, Pat drove us to Araluen for the Tulip Festival. Rose and I sat together in the back seats, and she chatted of old times.

In Canberra, we always meant to go to the Bowral Tulip Festival, but somehow never got there. Now, I indulged in a feast of flowers while Rose and I spoke of the many things left unsaid over the years, knowing it would most likely be our last meeting. Yet even then, neither of us mentioned our past quarrels lest we bring up old wounds again and break the magic spell now enveloping us.

I recalled the words of the American-Russian writer, Vera Nazarian, and remained silent. She has said, 'Siblings fight, pull each other's hair, steal stuff, and accuse each other indiscriminately. But siblings also know the undeniable fact that they are the same blood, share the same origins, and are family, even when they hate each other. And that tends to put all things in perspective.'

The festival was a delight to our senses. The perfume, the colours and the scenery exhilarated us. My sister and I had only one day left to be together, and I intended to make the most of it.

On Tuesday, our final day in Perth, Pat drove us to the Swan River to enjoy half an hour in an experimental driverless car. Before it arrived, Rose and I walked by the water opposite the island where Eileen had taken us for breakfast on Sunday. Once again, Rose poured out her heart. A feeling I had never had before for her flooded me. I had often failed to understand her. Now, I was filled with compassion and sorrow that frustration had led her to say so many hurtful and not quite truthful things. I began to realise how bravely she had borne her sufferings over the years. I realised, too, that the candle of understanding had been lit in my soul.

By the grace of God, Rose's two daughters had been instrumental in bringing us together.

On our flight back to Brisbane, I ruminated on Winston's behaviour in an effort to reconcile myself to his refusal to see me. *Why had he slipped into this morass of depression and not opened his door to us?* I reflected on his infant days. *How would he have felt when he had seen his mother being belted by his drunken father? How would he have felt when his beloved big brother Bertie had been driven from home and was no longer there to talk to or play with him? How would he have felt when I, his big sister who had looked after him in his infancy and as a toddler, left him to join a convent?*

Later, when Winston had moved to Australia, married, and had two girls, he had been again abandoned by his wife, who took their two children with her. He had been torn with grief, stopped playing his guitar, given up drink, but continued his karate and his work. After his retirement, he withdrew from society even further, and only allowed his youngest daughter to see him. He distanced himself from society and from his family. Although hurtful, I told myself it was his depression that had caused this distancing.

My heart bled for him. I have been lucky in my marriage. I thanked the Lord for all He has given me and prayed fervently for my loved ones. There was no point in imagining how things might have been had Winston opened the door and let us into his home, and his heart. The bond that linked me to my family was not only made of blood, but from the sharing of our joys and sorrows. However, my brother no longer wished to see me.

Chapter 27

Flooding, Fires and Ants, 2019

JANUARY 2019 BEGAN WITH PERFECT swimming weather. On weekends, we went to the beach rather than on the hills, as my right knee had been playing up, especially on a downhill slope. We would drive to the Southport Spit, north of Main Beach on the Gold Coast and find a place away from the colourful beach towels and giant umbrellas.

I loved to wriggle my toes in the sand and look at the waves crashing on the shore, or watch the burnt orange sunset bleed across the horizon. Colin would grab my hand, and we would run towards the water and splash through the incoming wavelets. He would release my hand in time to catch the outgoing swell that carried him into deeper water. I waded out into shoulder-deep water and immersed my head. When I rose and shook the water from my eyes, I searched for Colin and sighed with relief each time I spotted him, recalling the day we had been carried away by a rip.

A few years back, I had been enjoying myself, swimming in the shallow waters of Main Beach, Noosa, normally a safe beach patrolled by lifeguards. We frequented this spot often because of its calm waters and gentle waves. I enjoyed floating on my back and breathing in the smell of sea salt. I would listen to the waves crash on the rocky headland and relish the warm kiss of the setting sun. When swimming, I would stop every so often to check whether I had ventured into deeper water.

Life is full of surprises, not all of them welcome. On that day I stopped swimming to check the depth of the water and my distance from the shore. Suddenly, I was dragged off my feet. I fell forward, and thought I was being pulled under by a current. Straight away, I commenced to swim towards the shore, but made no progress. The ocean was dragging me out into the depths.

We had waited for the sun to set before entering the water, so the lifeguards had already packed up and gone. I panicked and went under. I could not touch the bottom, so I kicked and resurfaced.

Like a voice in the wilderness, Colin's voice drifted over the waters. 'Swim parallel to the shore. Towards the bay. We're caught in a rip.'

A rip! A strong narrow current that flows away from the beach... I tried to keep calm and, although exhausted, I kept going. Now I swam parallel to the shore rather than towards it. My lungs seemed about to burst. *How long can I keep swimming?*

The splash of water told me Colin had come to the rescue. He had succeeded in getting out of the rip, but I was still swimming, unaware that I too had emerged from its grasp. I coughed and sputtered, while Colin hauled me to my feet. We hugged each other before staggering to the beach.

That evening, I collapsed under the bedcovers, thanking God for holding His protective Hand over us. I did not realise that calm waters could be dangerous, but now, knowing the ocean's massive strength, I never take it for granted. Being caught in a rip and trying to swim to shore is like having your emotions in turmoil. You know in which direction you want your life to take, but you are exhausted trying to reach your goals.

Early in the year, an intense low-pressure system hung over Townsville, and major flooding occurred across the region. That inundation was one of the worst natural disasters ever to impact the region. Many locals volunteered to assist emergency services, by helping evacuate trapped residents from flooded homes. Later, they came to be known as the "tinny army". Something like the evacuation of Dunkirk during World War II, when every type of craft was used to save the trapped soldiers.

More than 500,000 head of cattle, already weakened from the drought, died during the disaster, but the floods brought stricken communities closer to each other. When our local church collected donations for the flood victims, we did our bit, knowing it was but a drop in the mighty ocean of suffering.

Meanwhile, further south, life continued as normal. The prospect of knee replacement surgery kept nagging me. I wanted to be fit again, so in early February Colin took me to an orthopaedic surgeon, who told me I needed total knee replacements, and handed me a booklet of the pros and cons of the procedure.

After reading it, I said, 'I don't think I'd like to risk having an operation.'

Colin agreed, but wanting a second opinion, he searched the web for surgeons who specialised in knee surgery and made an appointment for me. We saw the surgeon in March. His policy was: 'No pain, no operation.'

I was not on painkillers because my knees hurt only when going downhill, and since I only used the drugs when hiking on hills, we decided I did not need an operation, and concentrated on exercise to strengthen my muscles.

Colin bought a portable exercise bike and, as my walking improved, he also bought me a Sky Walker cross trainer. Although both the specialists had commented on my lack of cartilage in the joints as *bone on bone*, my knees showed signs of improvement, and I suffered less discomfort when going downhill.

Every spring, I suffered allergies from pollens, but in September this year my coughing increased alarmingly. The doctor suspected a 'B' flu virus, took a swab from my throat, and sent it off to the pathologist. It turned out to be a respiratory infection, and not influenza as he had suspected.

My cough and shortness of breath continued till the end of October and left me exhausted from the slightest exertion. Colin did all the shopping, cooking and housework. Although we had consulted a respiratory specialist the previous year, Colin decided to get a second opinion, and took me to another doctor, who sent me for a series of blood tests, x-rays and CT scans. I even had an echocardiogram in case I had a heart problem.

After all these tests, the doctor said, 'You don't have lung cancer or heart problems,' and put me on a steroid puffer for my shortness of breath.

I had never suspected lung cancer, but he wanted to make sure that my asthma was brought on by allergies and not something more serious. I used the steroid puffer for a while and continued with my exercises. We also resumed our bush walks but avoided hilly areas. My breathing problems slowly decreased, so I weaned myself off the drugs, knowing they can cause liver and kidney problems, high blood pressure, heart attack or stroke. Besides all this, they can bring on psychological symptoms like mood swings, delusions, or paranoid jealousy. Mental conditions already existed in my family, so I was not game to risk either my physical or mental health.

We spent much of the first six months of 2019 in doctors' surgeries. Studying for the Orchid Judges' Course also took up a great deal of time. Because of this, my writing suffered, and my creative juices dried up. The first half of the year went by with no speaking events except for the Carindale Writers' Group's launch of our anthology, *Nail Biters*.

Then in early July, it was announced that *The Sides of Heaven* was one of three finalists in the Australia and New Zealand-wide CALEB Competition of 2019. When I heard the news, I sobbed with joy. Its prequel, *Heaven Tempers the Wind: Story of a War Child* had also been a finalist in the 2017 CALEB Competition. It was too good to be true. Being a finalist once could have been a fluke. Twice was a miracle. Ecstasy bore me up on the wings of joy.

At the end of July, the Palm Beach Library, where we convened our monthly writers' meetings, invited our writing group to a Creative Artists' Show. I spent the day with two other authors. Crowds rolled up, and we sold several books.

Late in September, my publisher Rochelle Manners of Rhiza Press, held a whole day conference for her authors at the Fiction Bar, Raby Bay. We enjoyed sharing our knowledge with fellow authors and met many new and old friends. A spirit of camaraderie prevailed.

On Saturday 20 October, the Capalaba Library invited me to the Authors' Expo to display my books and give a talk. It was only a five-minute session, unlike the longer ones I had given the previous year, but I was grateful for every opportunity.

While sickness took its toll and increased my stress levels, Colin's stress also escalated. Not only did he worry about my health and take me to medical appointments, but his orchids suffered from a plague of ants. An infestation of mealy bugs followed. The hours he spent spraying his orchids and re-potting them are too many to count. But there is no success without stress, and we struggled on.

Southern Queensland had escaped the floods that the northern region had suffered earlier. However in the first week of September, one of the worst bushfires in history broke out. Fuelled by prolonged dry conditions and fierce winds, the Gold and Sunshine Coasts as well as the grape-growing town of Stanthorpe turned into blazing furnaces. The fire front spread to Lamington National Park and ravaged the heritage-listed Binna Burra Lodge. It had only one narrow access road, so firefighters abandoned the area and fled from the blaze.

On weekends we had gone for bush walks in National Parks. Tears moistened my eyes when television channels displayed photos of a rescued koala and her joey seated on a burnt log. She had huddled up to protect the joey in her pouch. Now she sat on the log with singed fur, raw patches of burnt flesh and blistered paws. Sympathy brought compassion, but when I heard of the koala's death a few days later, I suffered a visceral connection, and sobs tore through my body. Like so many of our heroic firefighters, the mother had saved her joey's life at the cost of her own.

Firies have been haunted by the dying screams of koalas. I too have had nightmares of the burned koala with her joey.

Fires incinerated most of the wildlife. Others suffocated from the smoke. Wombats panic at the smell of smoke and, when cut off from their burrows, the small stubby-legged marsupials run from the burning inferno. After 30 kilometres, they collapse from exhaustion and are consumed by the blaze or fall prey to feral cats and red foxes that await their prey on the fire front.

If they escape from the tongues of fire and the fangs of predators, they make a mad dash across a road. People unknowingly run over the poor wombats with their cars. The survivors are then attacked by domestic dogs or cats.

After the fire, the remaining wildlife return, only to find their habitat and food sources destroyed.

While the fires raged, Colin and I would have morning and afternoon tea beneath the shade of our pecan tree. One day he said, 'Did you hear about the beef farmer who says that wombats save the lives of wildlife?'

I knew he would not have the heart to joke about our wildlife during such a stressful time, so I put down my coffee and gave him my full attention. 'How do they do that?'

'They dig wells as deep as four meters in their burrows during droughts and allow other wildlife to shelter with them.'

'How do we know this?' I asked.

'A farmer set up a camera just outside a burrow and saw birds, butterflies, goannas, possums and echidnas enter the burrow to drink from the four-meter-deep well.'

'How astonishing! Hope no foxes or other predators get in too.'

'The wombat watches out for predators and kills them.'

I imagined the bloody battle between them and wondered whether it would be a fair match.

'The wombat curls himself into a ball and when the fox walks over him he raises himself by his powerful hind legs and crushes the fox's body against the roof of his cave.'

'They are so strong and yet so hospitable. I love them even more than I've ever done.'

Fires bring out the best in people too. Networks of community care centres arose. Locals and animal care centres took the burnt and sick animals into their care, and well-wishers from overseas sewed hammocks and pouches for young koalas or kangaroos or knitted nests for wounded birds. Closer to home, the Irwin family sheltered numbers of injured animals in their zoo's Wildlife Hospital that specialised in treating koalas, our beloved furry marsupials.

Like iron is made stronger by the fiercest flames, during bushfires, people showed their moral fibre and a true spirit of mateship by helping their friends and neighbours.

In November, New South Wales and Victoria also burst into flames. Fortunately for Queensland, 20 mm to 40 mm of rain fell, giving firefighters a brief respite, but forests and farms continued to blaze in Gippsland. Western Australia, Tasmania and South Australia were not spared either. I recalled the avenue of lime trees leading into the camping grounds at Buchan in Victoria, and thought of our happy times there. My heart bled for the inhabitants: both human and animals in fire-ravaged areas. On Kangaroo Island, thousands of koalas died in the fire. Kangaroo Island has been referred to as Noah's Ark because it contained many endangered species of wildlife, introduced to the island when the koala population of the mainland declined. Now so many of them, along with other endangered species, perished.

The whole of Australia suffered from the infernos. Questions have arisen about the feasibility of hazard-reduction burning, when nature is scarified, not atomised, like the original inhabitants of Australia had been doing for years. Perhaps these unprecedented conflagrations would not have occurred to such a vast extent had we continued our former hazard-reduction burning policy.

While firefighters toiled endlessly throughout the Christmas period, the lucky ones living in areas free from the flames, celebrated together and rejoiced in the fellowship of friends. A neighbour invited the whole street to join in their festivities, and all those who could go were there. It was a pleasure to meet old acquaintances and greet new ones.

Colin and I attended Christmas celebrations at both our Orchid and Writing Clubs, but nothing could top the lunch we had on

Christmas Day at our neighbours Maggie and Mike's home with traditional roast turkey and all the trimmings. The lovely Christmas tree, the decorations and delicious meal took me back to my early childhood days, and joy filled my heart. The fires all around Australia were still burning, but we looked heavenward and prayed for wet weather.

The decade ended with fire engulfing the land. Smoke shrouded large swathes of our country. Holiday makers huddled on beaches for safety, and ash particles thickened the air, making every breath a fight for life.

The Clyde Mountain fire between Batemans Bay and Braidwood placed both towns in danger. Fires threatened communities in the Snowy Mountains, Bega Valley, and the south coast from Nowra to Lakes Entrance in Victoria. We had spent many happy weekends at Eden during the early years of our marriage. I grieved on recalling the wonderful days we had there and the bakery that sold the best hot cross buns.

The weather bureau forecast rain in New South Wales and Victoria by the end of January. *Would that be too late? How many acres of Australia would lie waste by then? How many homes destroyed, trees, bushes, plants and wildlife incinerated, and human lives lost?*

Worry is a rocking chair that moves but gets nowhere, and all our worrying was unable to prevent an even bigger disaster in the succeeding months.

Chapter 28

Panic, 2020

ON 11 JANUARY 2020, CHINA REPORTED the first death from coronavirus. A man returning from Wuhan on January 25 brought the virus into Australia. Then Chinese students returning to Australia after celebrating the lunar New Year in their hometowns also spread the infection. At that stage, there was no known antidote or vaccine for it, so hospitals could only dose patients on antivirals, antibiotics, anti-inflammatories and anti-coagulants, or give them oxygen to ease their breathing. When the pandemic reached our shores, people thought it heralded the end of the world.

In early February, because people feared supplies could run out due to the closure of factories in mainland China, Hong Kong supermarkets ran out of long-lasting food items and hygiene products. Soon after, supermarket shelves across the world emptied as panic-buying began. In Australia, essential foodstuffs like bread, flour and rice, canned beans, tomatoes, pasta, pasta sauce, bottled water, toilet paper and hand sanitisers disappeared from stores.

The shortage of goods in Australia reminded me of the time British forces retreated from Burma in 1942. People panicked. Those intending to remain until Britain retook the country stocked up on supplies. I recall my father buying substantial quantities of rice, oil, tinned provisions. Unfortunately, Japanese planes bombed the town where we had taken refuge, forcing us to flee again. We loaded a pram with essentials like baby food, a blanket each and other essentials. Abandoning most of our food and clothes, we joined the hordes of refugees heading north to a village in the foothills of the Himalayas.

By mid-March, parents were receiving mixed messages about their children's safety in schools. The Federal government assured them students were not at risk. However, State governments encouraged children to remain at home. By the last week of Term 1, schools closed for the Easter break, as well as for an additional two weeks.

Orchid club meetings as well as writers' meetings stopped. Colin and I accepted self-isolation willingly. Colin devoted more time to our orchids. On discovering many sick and ailing plants among our collection, he was able to give them all the care they needed.

I took the opportunity of concentrating on my writing, neglected because of our studies for the Orchid Judges' Course. My creative juices flowed again and inspired me to write with enthusiasm.

Despite worldwide deaths from the disease, on March 19, NSW allowed 2650 passengers to leave the cruise ship *Ruby Princess,* even though some passengers felt unwell. Others held a party at the Sails restaurant before departing for their respective homes. As a result, the number of infections linked to that ship alone escalated to 900.

COVID-19 is deadly because carriers are asymptomatic for days, and because people do not possess antibodies against this new virus. It is of a similar strain as the MERS and SARS coronaviruses, but so far, no vaccine had proved effective against it. The SARS virus broke out in 2003 in China and lasted six months, the 2015 MERS virus had ended in three months, but no one had any idea how long COVID-19 would last.

The Spanish flu pandemic of 1918, the deadliest in history, infected an estimated 500 million people worldwide—about a third of the planet's population—and killed about 20 to 50 million people. That pandemic lasted twelve months before it ended its deadly march.

Lockdowns started all over the world, and over a million jobs were lost. People shuddered in apprehension of the future.

COVID-19 also affected world markets. The travel industry, especially cruise travel, took the initial brunt of the downturn. Opera and other live performances came to a halt. Writers' festivals were cancelled. I had been looking forward to the Omega Conference in October, but that too, was cancelled.

Colin wore a frown as he poured himself a cup of coffee beneath shade of our pecan tree, and I knew he was ruminating over news from the BBC. 'Murray Gunn has compared the current financial situation to the Wall Street crash of 1929.'

'Who is Murray Gunn?'

'He's the head of global research at the market forecasting firm Elliott Wave International.'

'Does he predict one as big as the Great Depression of 1929?'

'Yes, but he says there'll be a short-lived bounce in the markets first. The rebound will be what we call a dead cat bouncing.'

I sighed with relief because we now held only a few shares in the market.

Opera, Orchids and Oz

Every cloud has a silver lining. Despite the disastrous outlook on world markets, pollution levels all over the world dropped. Because manufacturing industries in China stopped temporarily, the sky over China turned blue once more. In Venice, as cruise ships no longer docked at the port, canals resumed their beauty and sparkled with life.

Few Australians were spared from the desperate visions of the natural calamities of fires, floods and storms. January 2020 was the hottest month on record. Drought and heat brought ideal conditions for forest fires. Foliage exploded due to vapourised oil from the eucalyptus and proved an incentive for incendiaries. By the second week the inferno burned around 25 million acres of land, an area larger than South Korea or Portugal. Fires, which had started in September the previous year, destroyed hundreds of properties with multiple fatalities and killed more than a billion animals, including endangered species, across eastern and southern Australia.

Around 4000 people in Victoria wore safety goggles, scarves or protective masks and spent New Year's Eve huddled together on the beach at Mallacoota. Dead birds, blackened by the fires, were washed up on the shores of East Gippsland, 400 kilometres away.

In New South Wales, fires tore through the Blue Mountains. I recalled the delightful walks we had enjoyed there, and the famous Three Sisters who stood sentinel. We could almost smell the smoke, see the leaping and fast-moving flames, the water bombers, the exhausted firies, the wasted homes, and families left with nothing but the clothes on their backs.

I thought of the time when my family fled from the bombing of Katha by Japanese planes in 1942: the burned woman screaming and running along with a baby in her arms and a young child clinging onto her dress; her face a mess of tears. I knew how the victims of fire felt, and my heart shrivelled in sympathy.

On January 20, dust storms swept through regional New South Wales, smothering Dubbo and nearby towns. We had once visited the Dubbo zoo on our way down south. I wondered how the animals—both the incarcerated and wild ones—coped.

Damaging winds also swept through Queensland, bringing severe thunderstorms. A rain dump of 1.4 metres occurred over two weeks. Although the rain stamped out the remaining fires, the inundations wrecked homes and drowned livestock. However, the defence force managed to rescue cattle that had escaped to higher ground and were marooned on hilltops. In south-eastern Australia, hailstones the size of golf balls pelted down, smashing cars. Not far from us, flash flooding caused the temporary closure of the Movie World theme park.

While the downpours lashed the Australian mainland, Tasmania continued to remain in the grip of fires. Fire fighters, emergency services, doctors, nurses, paramedics and soldiers gave their best, but resources had been severely strained, so our Orchid Clubs raised money for the victims. Our Brisbane Species Club presented a thousand dollars to the Country Women's Association for the fire fighters, as some of them had lost their homes and even their lives while helping others.

Our own disruptions and inconveniences were minor by comparison. Due to the fires, most National Parks in Queensland had been closed in January, and because storms had triggered landslides, many of the parks stayed shut in February as well. However, by March, only Binna Burra National Park on the Gold Coast hinterland remained closed.

As soon as National Parks reopened, we drove to the Main Range National Park for a walk. Around Cunningham's Gap, nature was busy restoring the environment and blackened saplings were sending out fresh leaves. Everything looked green after the rains. The cheerful cries of bell birds sounded like a thousand fairies ringing tiny bells.

That weekend in March, the priest cleansed his hands with a hand sanitiser before distributing Holy Communion in church. He told the congregation, 'To protect you from the Coronavirus, no one will be allowed to drink wine from the Chalice, or kiss or shake hands when greeting each other.'

Surprised, we wondered why the Church had delayed two months before passing these regulations. Many of my friends had already stopped giving each other a peck on the cheek and satisfied themselves with a hug, although most men continued shaking hands at this stage.

Colin and I usually have a walk on Sundays when the weather is fine. On Sunday 14 March, we drove to the western part of Springbrook National Park. The mountains and hamlets lent an Arcadian atmosphere on our way to the Natural Bridge. Hoop Pines lined the easy 1.5 km circuit. The track took us up and around the awe-inspiring arch with its viewing spots of the waterfall and rock pools below.

The following Sunday, we drove to Spicer's Gap and passed through the Great Dividing Range, about four km south of Cunningham's Gap, named after the explorer, Alan Cunningham. In the 1800s, the road through the Gap proved negotiable for horses but unsuitable for loaded drays, because of the rockfall near the top. In 1847 Henry Alphen discovered a less arduous way via Spicer's Gap and, by 1857, teams of up to 60 bullocks pulled wool-laden drays through it.

Spicer's Gap Road was abandoned when the rail from Brisbane via Toowoomba to Warwick opened in 1871. Now, only picnickers and bushwalkers use it.

We hiked through eucalypt and sclerophyll forests, then through open grassy areas and scrambled over rocky outcrops on the rough Mount Mathieson Track. Even though only 8.5 km long, the trail led us up steep grades and down shale-covered slopes. It was the most challenging hike we had attempted since my pelvic fracture in 2017.

The Sunday we drove to Spicer's Gap was to be our last walk in a National Park for some time.

The following weekend Colin said, 'We'll go to Mount Barney National Park. We shouldn't meet many hikers there, as it is isolated.'

We packed our bushwalking gear and set out for the Scenic Rim, an arc of spectacular mountains stretching from Beaudesert to Ipswich. While enjoying a cup of coffee at a picnic area in Beaudesert, a man stopped a little distance from us. 'Please keep an eye on my dogs. I'm just going over to the shops.'

'We'll be here for another fifteen minutes,' Colin replied, and I nodded.

After our cup of coffee, we went to the next table to check on his dogs. They mounted guard on a blue and white plastic bag, the man's sole possessions. It struck me then that this homeless man had found a home wherever he went with his bags and two canine friends. Every little corner was his home.

Most of Mount Barney National Park is open eucalypt forest, with grassy slopes and tall spreading gums in the lower areas.

Creeks cascade into deep pools and flow through the park. The banks are lined with she oaks, golden silky oaks and red bottle brushes. Colourful kingfishers, honey eaters and robins, as well as a variety of other birds, flit from flower to flower and fill the air with their songs. We hoped to catch a glimpse of the elusive platypus that swim in the crystal-clear streams. Mount Barney is a World Heritage site. The iconic peak beckoned us as we neared our destination.

On our arrival, a prominent sign displayed the words, *'Park closed until further notice,'* in bold letters.

Swallowing my disappointment, I said, 'Where to now?'

'Let's try Lake Maroon,' Colin said. 'Perhaps we could do a few walks there.'

A five-minute drive took us to the vicinity of the lake but that was shut too.

Colin consulted a map of the area. 'Mount French National Park may be open.'

I fought back the impulse to bite my lip as we drove towards the park. Only short tracks meandered through the park, but it had a toilet and picnic tables, and was not far out of our way.

Once there, a sign indicated: *'All National Parks are now closed due to CORONA-19, and it is an offence to park cars or walk in the area.'*

Frustrated, we returned home and did some gardening. We had neglected it because of our studies for the orchid exam, which had been postponed due to COVID-19. It reminded me of the time when my exams were suspended just three months before I could complete my Arts Degree at the University of Rangoon, because of Civil War in Burma.

The following week, the government announced more stringent rules to contain the virus. Gatherings were restricted to two people, indoors and outdoors, and people were asked to keep 1.5 metres between each other. What hit us most was the closure of National

Parks. So, the first three months of 2020 ended on a sour note, leaving us dreading what the rest of the year would bring. But these challenges served to shape us. Not break us.

Chapter 29

April to August 2020

By the end of March, Australia had closed its borders, social distancing had been implemented, and non-essential surgery cancelled. Still, despite restricted international travel and border surveillance, on 2 April 2020, Australia had 269 new confirmed cases of COVID- 19. Therefore, rigid regulations came into force for the Easter weekend.

'In Jerusalem, the Church of the Holy Sepulchre, which was built on the site of Jesus's crucifixion, has closed for the first time since the Black Plague,' Colin said.

I placed my hand to my mouth. 'Then this pandemic must be as bad as the dreadful plague nearly 700 years ago.'

Because people were only allowed to go out for essential services and exercise, by Good Friday, 10 April 2020, Australia recorded less than a hundred new coronavirus infections for the first time in three weeks, with only 96 new infections in 24 hours.

We stayed home that day, frustrated because all church services had been cancelled. After watching an Easter Service on Channel 7, Colin looked up the latest news on the internet, then carried a tray with a coffee pot, sugar, oat milk, and two cups for morning tea in the garden. 'Border closures and social distancing has flattened the curve so far, but will we have another wave like the 1918 Spanish flu?'

'What caused the second wave?'

'When the war ended in 1918, crowds celebrated in the streets, kissing and hugging everyone,' Colin replied.

'Mum told me about all the celebrations on the streets. She had been a teenager then. Young and reckless.'

Colin nodded. 'More people died in the second outbreak than during the entire war.'

'Hope *we* don't get a second wave,' I said.

'The W.H.O. says that if restrictions are lifted too quickly, Wuhan will have a second wave of COVID by mid-year.'

Overawed by this dreadful news, I remained silent. COVID-19 had brought the whole world to its knees either in prayer or fear. *Will Australia relax social distancing laws now that the growth factor of the coronavirus is levelling out? Without constant vigilance, will we have another attack?*

Meanwhile, Colin and I googled walking tracks in the Redlands. To our surprise, we discovered several environmental reserves within 20 minutes from home. Each day, during the Easter season, we enjoyed two-hour walks in the Redlands area. Walking in local reserves gave us two advantages. We saved money on petrol and had more leisure time. Being sticklers for obeying the law, instead of spending an entire day in a National Park as we normally did, we only spent half a day at a local reserve. I was once told that I was a quintessential optimist, and my hopes for a speedy end to the virus still remained high.

At the beginning of April, numbers were still far below the death toll of the Spanish flu, but back then, no antibiotics were available to stem the lung infections caused by the virus.

'Hopefully, social distancing laws will be repealed for October, and we will have our Orchid Judges' Exam and perhaps even our spring orchid shows?' I enthused.

'Let's hope so,' Colin replied, but I saw the frustrated look in his eyes.

A week later, on Tuesday 21 April, as the case numbers dropped, Australians stranded overseas were flown back to Australian capital cities, but the state governments imposed a quarantine on the new arrivals. However, one of the inmates left the hotel via the fire escape stairs. He wedged the door open with a roll of toilet paper, so he could slip back into his room, unnoticed.

Because of this, restrictions remained in force. I stayed away from my general practitioner in case I was infected in the clinic, and excused myself from Writers' meetings unless they were held via ZOOM or Facebook. I flinched whenever someone coughed and hoped we would not catch the dreaded virus.

ANZAC Day went by with no marches and no large reunions. But we did not forget those who lost their lives in war. In the wee hours of the morning, people stood on their driveways to participate in the Dawn Service broadcast live across Australia by the ABC. We joined our neighbours at the top end of our street. Many held candles as we stood and listened to the service—physically separated, but not isolated.

Colin had experienced an ANZAC Dawn Service as a Sea Cadet in Portland, but I had never been to one. It had a profound effect upon me. I thought of all who had given their lives for king and country, and particularly of our ancestors who had fought and died in foreign lands.

A week later, in contrast to the restrictions on ANZAC Day, the Queensland Government announced that from the Labour Day weekend on May 2, people would be permitted to have picnics, bushwalks or leisurely drives. Some National Parks would be opened, but people would still only be allowed to travel within 50 km of their home.

Most National Parks are further than 50 kms from our home, so they still remained out-of-bounds to us.

'I feel like a prisoner in my own home,' Colin grumbled.

I shrugged my shoulders. 'But at least this lockdown has given you more time to tend to your orchids.'

'Yes. We were doing too much. It has given us the chance to take stock of our lives.'

Australia was still the Lucky Country in comparison to the rest of the world.

With the re-opening of some National Parks, Colin and I decided to go to Venman's Bushland National Park, one of the largest remaining areas of eucalypt forest in the Redland coastal lowlands. It is 40 kilometres south of Brisbane City, and home to koalas, sugar gliders, greater gliders, wallabies and possum. Frogs, water rats and eastern water dragons live around the creeks. The main tracks are Tingalpa Creek Circuit, which is only 2.5 km, and Venman Circuit, a reasonable hike of 7.5 km. Mountain bikes and horses are not permitted, so it is a peaceful area. We strolled along, enjoying the fresh air and the humming of birds, praising the Lord for keeping our environment safe.

After trialling less stringent measures over the Labour Day weekend, Queensland recorded five new cases of COVID-19 overnight. Our hopes of a speedy stop to the virus plunged into the lowest depths.

Despite the increase in cases worldwide, four Qantas planes left for India to rescue 500 Australians. Will that result in a second wave of the virus in Australia?

The Black Lives Matter protests held around the world when George Floyd died at the hands of a police officer in Minneapolis ignited rallies in Australia. On the first weekend of June, 30,000 Queenslanders marched through Brisbane's streets in protest of indigenous deaths in police custody. Huge crowds also gathered in other cities worldwide. These gatherings violated the law, but it was impossible to restrain them.

Schools reopened in June after a long break. I was glad I was no longer teaching. A friend told me how difficult things had been as she had to continue teaching the pupils who attended school as well as provide work for those who were studying on-line.

By the third week of June, the number of new coronavirus cases rose to 20, and in our area alone, two new infections were reported.

During the last week of June, Victoria had 16 new cases of COVID-19, so the Victorian Premier, who had just been considering winding down state restrictions on personal mobility, now wound back their freedom. People were aware that if the new outbreak rose to double figures, strict lockdown measures would remain in force for Victorians. An exodus began to NSW whose borders remained open, while Queensland, WA, SA, Tasmania and NT still had their borders closed. The Queensland Premier announced that our state borders would not be re-opened before September 2020, and people could not visit relatives who lived interstate. Not even for weddings or funerals. The number of calls to mental helplines like Beyond Blue and Lifeline increased by 50% during this period.

When the 50 km limit was lifted, Colin and I went further afield to Noosa National Park, our favourite coastal park in Queensland. We left our car at the southern end and commenced our 12 km round trip to the picnic area, where we intended to stop for lunch. The fresh air imbued us with new life and energy. The freedom to enjoy nature was a physical necessity and the walk was rewarding and joyful.

From July 3, restrictions were eased, and a maximum of 100 people could congregate in buildings and public spaces. Travel was permitted to anywhere in Queensland and overnight stays allowed.

Friends took advantage of this by travelling to the coast or out west to mining towns like Emerald and Rubyvale. We had been planning to visit these places too but had postponed our holiday because of COVID-19 restrictions. Now, our Orchid Judges' exam loomed ahead, and we could not spare any time for travel. However, we rejoiced as we could now attend church services.

On Saturday 4 July, a member of the church committee greeted us, pumped a few drops of sanitiser on our fingers, and directed us to our seats. Chairs were placed the recommended distance apart. Even members of the same household sat separately, but we were happy to be at our local church after so long.

The next day, we drove through Warwick and on to Killarney, until we reached Queen Mary's Falls in the Main Range National Park near Warwick. We had chosen Queen Mary's Falls as it was it was further from the City Centre than the National Parks on the Gold Coast hinterland, and we hoped to have a quiet stroll. To our surprise, the car park was full and the overflow were parked along the roadside for miles.

'We'll just have to park here and walk to the falls,' Colin said.

I nodded. 'The whole of Warwick and Killarney must be here.'

'I suppose they have no choice. It's either meet friends at a coffee shop or take your family for a picnic.'

We exchanged our shoes for hiking boots and buckled on our packs, then set out. The spot is part of the Gondwana Rainforests of Australia's World Heritage Area. We headed for the Queen Mary

Falls Circuit to explore the area where Spring Creek tumbles 40 metres to the valley below. The views were spectacular and the walk exhilarating. Many other hikers had taken advantage of the lovely weather and we found it almost impossible to keep the social distancing rules. Angry and frustrated, I said, 'We've driven all the way out here to try and get away from crowds.'

Colin, who had chosen this spot in an effort to abide by distancing rules, merely shrugged and drove on to Killarney for a picnic lunch. The peaceful atmosphere calmed my irritated nerves.

On returning home, we heard of the devastating surge of infection in Victoria, with 108 new cases reported. Our hearts went out to the people there. Soon, the Victorian borders shut down to prevent the spread of the pandemic. The second wave had reached our shores.

August had always been a lucky month for our family. In August 1952, we had gained liberty from our cruel father when we had fled from his clutches to a convent in Mandalay. In August 1967, I had left Burma for Australia to find freedom from the tyranny of a socialist and repressive government. In August 1970, Colin had proposed to me. Now, in August 2020, Colin and I passed our Orchid Judges' Exam.

My joy was not yet over. Before the month ended, Armour Books accepted my story of Colin's memoir for publication. My happiness spilled over. Even during these doubtful times, *Count Your Blessings: Colin's Story* was expected to be released in September. I spent the next few days frantically proofreading the PDF copy and deciding whether the selected book cover was suitable. Finally, we decided on one and, overwhelmed by joy, I requested my library for a date to launch the book.

Things slowly improved on the home front in the war against COVID. The number of guests in homes had been increased, and Queenslanders hoped that restrictions would soon be lifted despite the second outbreak in Victoria. Our hopes were shattered when on Monday 24 August, a prison worker tested positive to the virus after working at the Brisbane Youth Detention Centre in Wacol.

Strict restrictions were reimposed when six people linked to the Centre tested positive. Some of them came from Forest Lake, Ipswich and Carindale. Soon a breakout of the virus occurred at a gymnasium in Birkdale. As a result, homes across Greater Brisbane as well as outdoor gatherings were restricted to ten people. As we did not socialise much, these restrictions did not affect our lifestyle. But we were all in God's Hands.

Chapter 30

September to December 2020

Winter had thrown off its cloak of fog and spring was weaving a fresh green mantle. It was mid-week in September, and sun shone on the new growth where a bushfire had blazed earlier in the year. Colin and I hiked through open forest on the Witches' Falls Circuit in Mount Tamborine. Large boulders protruded on the steep slopes—huge jaws waiting to devour anyone daring to venture within reach.

We had been on this track several times, but dry weather had eroded much of the soil and exposed rocks of varying heights, making the normally easy walk more difficult than usual. I took particular care when traversing this treacherous terrain as the cartilage in my knees were worn down to nothing. I was still putting off that double knee replacement.

We zig-zagged down the mountain, carefully picking our way over weather-worn rocks. Despite my two hiking poles, I lost my balance, stumbled, and involuntarily ran downhill. The force of gravity drew me like a magnet to the edge of the cliff, where the weather-beaten soil was unstable. It gave way beneath my feet. I fell headlong, my right side taking the brunt of the fall. Helpless, I rolled down the slope. *Was this the end?* I breathed a prayer as I slid towards the ravine.

Suddenly I stopped tumbling, and lay on my back, facing heavenward. I remained still, afraid to move lest I started plunging down again. Everything was silent. I took deep breaths and tried to gain a foothold on a clump of three saplings by stretching my feet towards them, but they were beyond my reach.

The thud of boots told me that Colin was racing to rescue me. 'I'm all right, darling,' I shouted, hoping he would slow down and not fall. Colin ran past and stopped below me in case I started rolling once more. I heard him kicking away the loose soil, and knew he was attempting to gain a firm foothold.

Within minutes, he stood beside me, looking down anxiously at my prone figure.

'I need something to brace my foot against and help me get up.'

'Brace yourself against me.'

'But you may roll down.'

'No. I have planted my feet on solid ground and can support you.'

I rolled over, used my arms to lever myself up, and rose to my knees. I attempted to crawl up the slope, but the soil kept giving way and I slid back. Fortunately, Colin stayed immediately behind me. I used his booted foot to gain a firm footage, then scrambled up the hill on all fours. His firm stance on the terrain and his mere presence gave me renewed energy. I grasped shrubs and rocks to pull myself up, but I skidded back time and time again.

A rock gave way beneath my grasp and rattled down the shaley surface. How far down was the bottom? We could not see it from the track. *It must be very steep! Will Colin be able to support me if the soil gives way and I keep slipping? Will my weight dislodge his feet and precipitate us both downhill? Will our mangled bodies reach the foot of the mountain?* I thought of 'Lovers' Leap,' where two lovers had leapt to their fate. Where did I hear of it? The Gap. In Sydney. My throat was dry. My lips parched. My strength failing.

I raised my head to measure how much further we had to climb. The track was only a few metres away. Hope revived me, replenishing my diminished muscle force. With one more gigantic effort, I pulled on a sapling, and finally reached the top.

As soon as I out of danger, Colin sprang like a panther upon the path. We hugged each other in silence, then I sat on a rock and surveyed the scene. I had rolled down a 45-degree incline for about four or five meters.

'You were only a couple of meters away from a 60-degree drop,' Colin pointed out.

'It was a miracle I didn't keep hurtling down.'

'It *seems* like one,' Colin said. 'But perhaps the slope plateaued out before the sharp plunge and stopped you.'

I suffered no serious injury. No broken bones, torn tendons, or muscles. A thorn from a lantana bush was embedded in my right forefinger, and I had a nasty bruise on the same hand. Nothing to worry about. I could have broken my neck or my back in the fall or dislocated a limb. I could have died. *This is nothing short of a miracle,* I thought.

Once again, God had sent Colin to rescue me. I recalled the number of times he saved me from all kinds of scrapes, big and small. The first time was at Luna Park in Sydney. We had gone for a ride in a rotating barrel known as the Rotor, not long after my coma. When the Rotor stopped, everyone was told to disembark but, dizzy from the spinning, I could only hang on to the sides, until Colin came in, and led me out before the Rotor took off again.

The second time he saved me was when I failed to return from that orienteering session.

I again thanked the Lord for my miraculous escape.

After my ordeal on Tamborine Mountain, everything looked peaceful. We continued our walk in silence. The sun shone and the perfume of jasmine from the nearby cemetery wafted towards us. Life was wonderful. It seemed incredible that only moments before my life had been in jeopardy.

Over the years, we had climbed steeper mountains and hiked over more rocky terrain. Only six months' ago, we had done the rough Mount Mathieson Track at Spicer's Gap in the Main Range National Park, a really tough climb up steep grades and down shale-covered slopes, and I had come away without a fall or a scratch. Although thankful to God for saving me from serious injury, I felt embarrassed for having fallen on a comparatively easy walk.

The profound silence was broken by the sound of a kookaburra cackling. Was it laughing at me?

The day after my accident, I visited my chiropractor who worked on my neck, back and arms, leaving me as good as new. He remarked how lucky I was to have escaped more serious injury.

Next morning, I received an email from Tabor College in South Australia, informing me that my short story, *An Angel in Heaven Now*, had been selected for publication in their 2020 Stories of Life Anthology and it was also being considered for a prize. Overjoyed, I passed the news on to my friends. That month, a dear neighbour invited us and a few other friends to celebrate the release of my latest book, *Count Your Blessings: Colin's Story*. It was such a pleasure to meet and exchange news. I came away breathing in the sweet smell of success and still relishing the taste of delicacies on my tongue.

By mid-September, tired of restrictions, some writing groups resumed face-to-face meetings at members' homes or coffee clubs. Three of our orchid clubs, too, held monthly meetings, but kept social distancing rules. We entered our names on a sheet for the Department of Health and sanitised our hands. We had gone through a riot of changes in the previous six months. The simple life of isolation had been quite liberating, and Colin and I had learned to love this period of enforced restriction.

Normality seemed strange. I was overwhelmed at the partial return to normal life. Like a zombie, I did everything mechanically and found it difficult to put names to faces. Most members of the orchid clubs and writing groups wore forced smiles and had strained looks. I am sure I, too, displayed the same baffled look.

A month later, when we attended our next meeting, I was already beginning to feel more relaxed. To my surprise, two orchid judges congratulated me. One said, 'Congratulations for joining the judging world.'

Another said, 'So you're now an Associate Judge. Congratulations!'

It made my day. All those months on study had paid off. Colin and I were Associate Judges after two years of hard work. If we could make it through another three years of practical work, we will be internationally recognized Orchid Judges.

While we were enjoying greater freedom, relatives in the UK emailed to say that Colin's cousin Geoff had died. None of them could attend the funeral because Nottingham was in strict lockdown. In fact, it had the highest number of coronavirus cases in the United Kingdom.

Geoff, the eldest of all the cousins, had been only a couple of months older than Colin. His sudden death came as a shock and increased our anxiety for the relatives back in England. All we could do was to pray for their safety. It aroused our awareness of life's fragility, and even though Geoff's death was not due to COVID-19, I wondered how many of us would survive the pandemic.

Soon after, Colin's sister from Maryborough phoned to say that Aunt Barbara, who had been in a nursing home for several years, had passed away. Funerals were still restricted to only a few people, so not many were able to pay their respects in person. I recalled the funerals I had attended when the sole comfort for families was to hug each other, while sobs tore their bodies. The sense of touch, the clasp of a hand or merely the ability to sit together in silence brought solace to their sufferings, but now, even this was being denied.

We were overcome by sorrow at not being able to join the mourners at Aunt Barbara's funeral. All we could do was to send a floral wreath.

Rose and her two daughters as well as my brother Winston and his daughters were comparatively safe in Perth. Rose kept in touch via emails and Winston still lived in seclusion, so although he still did not respond to contact, I knew the lockdown would scarcely affect him. I guessed that Rose, however, would miss her travels and would not take to the restrictions easily. I prayed for them.

Early in November, the British Broadcasting Station announced that a 91-year-old grandmother had been given the first Pfizer COVID-19 jab as part of a mass vaccination programme. It was the first of 8,000,000 doses of the vaccine dispensed in the coming weeks. The over 80s, health care workers and care staff were given the highest priority.

'Will we take the vaccines if they are released here?' I asked Colin when we heard the news.

'Only if it is compulsory. I hope it will not be the Chinese vaccine that has been trialled in the Middle East and only been approved by the United Arab Emirates. The UAE says it is 86% reliable, but I have my doubts.'

'Yes. I believe that even the UK ones are not recommended for those with allergy problems,' I said.

'True. The medical regulatory agency has said that vaccinations should not be carried out in facilities that do not have resuscitation equipment.'

'Well, at least we're on the way to finding effective vaccines,' I said. 'I'm sure 2021 will see the end of the pandemic.'

The future looked brighter not only for the world, but for my writing career. Early in December, two of my stories were published in the 2020 Carindale Writers' Group anthology. Colin and I were at the launch. It was a more subdued affair than previous years, but the group were able to celebrate 20 years of achievement since its foundation by Beverley Asmus.

That month, my short story, *An Angel in Heaven Now* was also published in Tabor's 'Stories of Life' anthology. The book launch was in South Australia and I was overjoyed to receive a copy of the anthology.

Before the year ended, the superyacht, *Lady E*, docked in Cairns, with an infected crew on board, brought COVID-19 into our state again on December 21. As did a Queenslander returning home after visiting Sydney's Northern Beaches, one of NSW's hotspots. As a result, a major scare arose, and the premier ordered the shutdown of our borders once again.

The closure affected many of our friends, who had been planning get-togethers with family across Australia. Colin and I had no plans for a reunion in Perth, but Colin's relatives sent us emails lamenting their inability to celebrate with families scattered all over the UK. They were still in lockdown.

On Christmas Eve, Colin said, 'A Brexit deal has finally been agreed between the UK and the EU.'

'That will bring some consolation to your English cousins,' I said.

Colin nodded. 'Now the UK will not be under European law. Besides, there's a free trade deal with zero quotas and zero tariffs.'

'What about Scotland, Northern Ireland and Wales?' We had been aware of the discontent, and both of us wanted Great Britain to remain united.

'Wales says it's better than no deal. Scotland says it is happening against their will, and Ireland thinks it represents a good compromise and a balanced outcome.'

'Well, that's not too bad, is it? Perhaps the UK will remain united,' I said, calling to mind the adage, *United we stand. Divided we fall.*

That Christmas, we spent more time with friends and neighbours. Early in December, we had lunch and afternoon tea with a couple from an orchid club and before the week ended, the four of us had dinner with another couple from the same club. Colin and I dined out with friends from a writing group and had meals at cafés with my other writing groups to celebrate Christmas.

As the holiday season drew nearer, neighbours invited us to join their festivities. COVID-19 brought us closer to each other. Christmas and Boxing Day passed at the home of our dear friends Maggie and Mike with a scrumptious dinner. With such delightful company and a houseful of Christmas cheer, how could we be anything but joyful?

So, 2020 ended on a happy note. The seeds of the final volume of my memoirs, *Opera, Orchids and Oz*, as well as my historical novel, *The Soprano*, were still in the soil, but I trust they will bear good fruit. In February next year, I also hoped to celebrate my Golden Wedding Anniversary with my husband, Colin, my beloved companion these past years through joy and sorrow, pain and ecstasy, the good and the bad.

I approached the end of the year with gratitude to the Lord for all the blessings He has bestowed upon us, granting us a happy marriage, giving me health despite my near-death experience in the early days of our marriage, and letting me fly away with Colin to the ends of the world—and finally fulfilling of my dream of being an author. Above all, I praise the Lord for giving us the gifts of Faith and Hope.

Epilogue

My brother, Winston, tried to end his life by taking an overdose of antihistamines on our mother's birthday, 12 November 2021. My sister, Rose, his niece, Eileen, and two daughters, Tania and Sheree, found him face down in his sitting room, and sent for an ambulance.

Fortunately, Winston failed in his attempt. He remained in hospital for a month. During his stay there, he would answer my phone calls, and speaking to him again was like hearing the *Hallelujah Chorus*.

After a month's treatment at Fremantle Hospital, Winston was sent to a mental hospital for a psychological assessment. Then a team of psychiatrists allowed him home for the weekend provided he promised not to try to terminate his life again. Once out, Winston discharged himself from hospital and has been living at home ever since. He has not replied to my phone calls, but I pray and hope he will never attempt to end God's gift of life, but to wait until he is called to a better world.

Also by Hazel Barker

Heaven Tempers the Wind: *Story of a War Child*
Finalist CALEB Awards 2017

The Sides of Heaven
Finalist CALEB Awards 2019

The Chocolate Soldier: *Story of a Conchie*

Count Your Blessings: *Colin's Story*
Finalist CALEB Awards 2021

www.ingramcontent.com/pod-product-compliance
Lightning Source LLC
Chambersburg PA
CBHW021142080526
44588CB00008B/175